Connect
with Nature

Projects to grow, gather,
make and do

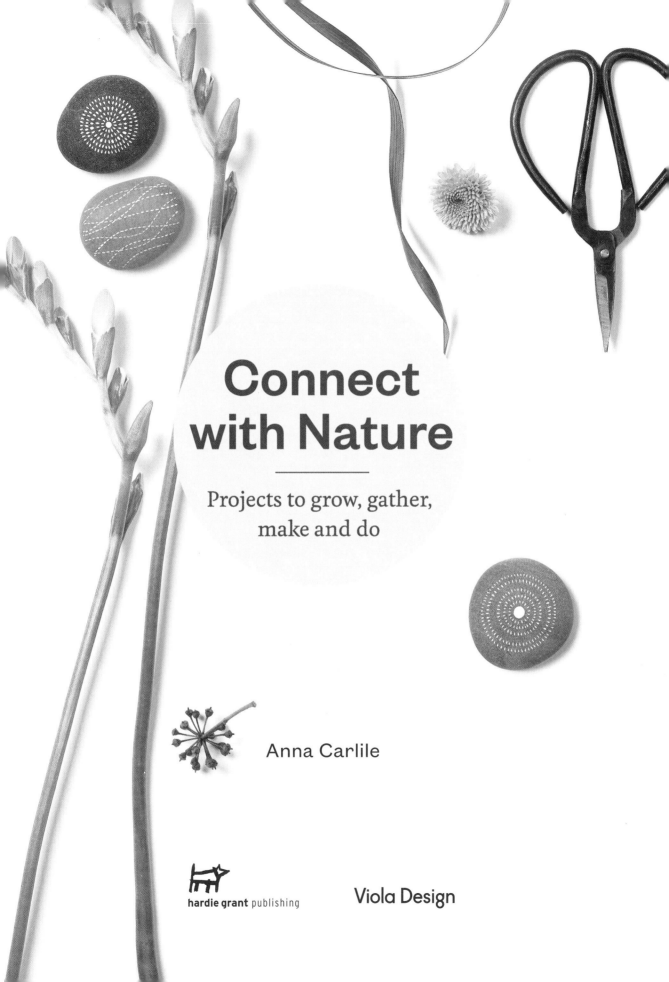

Connect with Nature

Projects to grow, gather, make and do

Anna Carlile

hardie grant publishing

Viola Design

"Live in each season as it passes;
breathe the air, drink the drink, taste
the fruit, and resign yourself to the
influence of the earth."

— HENRY DAVID THOREAU, *WALDEN*

Contents

Anna Carlile is the founder of Viola Design,
a communication design company that draws
inspiration from nature and promotes design
which celebrates and protects the environment.
She lives in Melbourne, Australia with her partner
Nick and two children, Tasman and Freya.

Connect with Nature is born from Anna's own
desire to balance the tension of wanting to live in
the city, with its exciting fusion of ideas, vibrancy,
art and culture, and wanting to immerse herself
in the spaciousness and beauty of nature.

Connect with Nature enables us to have the best
of both worlds. Anna has researched, compiled
and tested a range of nature-inspired projects
and activities that offer you ways to live in the
city and connect with nature every day.

Introduction

Slow down. Simplify. Let go.

Connect with Nature does just this. It's your entry into a world that spins slowly and draws its inspiration from the earth, the ocean, the sun and the sky.

Whether you live in an apartment, have a small patch of urban greenery, or an expansive jungle at your door, the seasonal projects and activities in *Connect with Nature* reveal the ways you can weave creativity, the environment and wild fun into your everyday life.

Walk in nature, climb a tree, make a kite and go fly it. Sprout your own seeds, grow herbs, dig for clay, paint stones and read the different phases of the moon. Be guided by the stars, watch the sunrise, smell the rain.

You'll get your hands dirty, feel the sand beneath your feet, the wind in your hair and reconnect with days of old and childhoods past. Put down the devices and let your only connectivity be with nature, your friends, family, and, of course, yourself.

Connect with Nature is your portal to an unhurried, unstructured, unencumbered connection - so throw open the doors and let nature in.

SPRING

go outside

———

"Nature holds the key to our aesthetic, intellectual,
cognitive and even spiritual satisfaction."

— EDWARD O. WILSON

Start a veggie patch

With spring comes renewed light and warmth, and the promise of abundance. It's the season for emerging from wintry hibernation, and starting afresh. To welcome the season, start your own veggie patch and watch the fruits of your labor flourish throughout the year into food for your table.

GATHER TWO BAGS OF QUALITY TOPSOIL / NEWSPAPER, CARDBOARD OR OLD CARPET / MIXED SEEDS AND SEEDLINGS OF YOUR CHOICE / TWO BAGS OF MUSHROOM COMPOST / TWO BAGS OF COW MANURE / ADDITIONAL COMPOST FROM YOUR GARDEN / ONE BALE OF LUCERNE OR PEA STRAW / POLYPIPE HOOPS, SHADE CLOTH, PEST NETTING AND CLEAR PLASTIC (OPTIONAL)

It's time to head outside and get your hands dirty by creating a vegetable garden. Previous generations dug their vegetable patches straight into the garden – a labor of love that involved lots of bending and kneeling. These days, raised garden beds are commonplace, as the extra height depth means healthier, deeply rooted plants, and better backs and knees for gardeners (there will also be less weeding down the track).

Ready-made raised garden beds are available from nurseries and hardware stores. If you're feeling particularly do-it-yourself, source some recycled planks of wood from your local tip and build your own. A garden bed is easy enough to hammer together if you have all the tools (a drill and some screws should do it) and a simple 200 x 100 cm (79 x 39 in) rectangle is a great place to start.

Your bed should sit at around knee height – otherwise you're going to need a ladder to harvest your climbing beans and tomatoes. The higher your bed goes, the narrower it needs to be. This is for ease of access, and also to optimise soil use and drainage.

Where to put your veggie patch

Before you start planting your vegetable garden, you'll need to decide on the location of your garden bed. If you only have a small urban garden, then nestling it up against a fence in a sheltered sunny spot is ideal.

You want to make sure your garden bed is protected from winds and frost, receives adequate sun during the cooler seasons, and not too much sun during the hotter seasons. It's also wise to keep your garden close to the kitchen for easy access to herbs and produce.

Setting up your garden bed

1. Locate your garden bed in your preferred location, and line the bottom of the bed thickly with recycled newspaper, cardboard or a piece of old carpet to suppress any weeds or grass.

2. As an optional step, create a structure to support pest netting or a shade cloth by hammering in small stakes a few centimetres out from the four corners of your bed. You'll need to buy polypipe arches that fit neatly over your stakes to support the net. You can purchase a net from nurseries and hardware stores.

3. Fill your bed with a third each of quality topsoil, mushroom compost and cow manure. Use a gardening fork to mix them thoroughly. These are readily available from good nurseries and landscape suppliers. If you have any compost ready, by all means add that too. Regularly feeding your soil with fresh compost and green manure crops (such as plants in the pea and bean family) will keep it healthy and nutritious for your plants.

4. Now it's time for the fun part – planting with seasonal seeds and seedlings. If the weather is hot, early morning or evening is the best time to plant, as the seedlings will have time to settle in without being scorched by the sun. You can source a range of organic heirloom seeds and seedlings from nurseries. Consider availing yourself of a seasonal planting guide relevant to your location, and find out what experienced local gardeners are growing, and when. If you see a particularly nice garden, say hello and ask the owner for tips. Keep in mind the space requirements of your mature veggies when deciding how many to plant, and grow what you most enjoy eating. Give your seedlings a gentle soak and mulch with the pea straw or lucerne to retain moisture.

5. Once you've planted the first seeds in your new vegetable patch, use a calendar or notebook to keep track of when to harvest your spring vegetables, and to schedule when to plant your summer, fall and winter vegetables. You can also plan out tasks, such as adding more compost and manure to your garden bed, and when to turn your summer abundance into preserves to last you throughout the cooler months.

6. Continue to tend lovingly and enjoy your harvest.

Companion planting

Companion plants are the allies of the plant world – when planted next to each other in your garden bed, companion plants will help with pest control, improve taste and increase yield. Start with these popular companion plants and watch your garden grow:

• Basil helps tomatoes by repelling flies and mosquitoes and can improve the taste of your tomatoes.

• Catnip repels fleas, ants and rodents, and is great alongside most plants.

• Chives planted under roses will deter aphids and blackspot.

• French marigold is a fantastic companion plant for most vegetables as it kills root knot nematodes and eel worm.

• Garlic will deter aphids, especially on raspberries or roses.

• Nasturtiums can be planted near leafy vegetables, like lettuce, to draw caterpillars away.

• Rosemary repels carrot fly and therefore goes well with carrots.

• Sunflowers planted with corn will increase the yield, and attract ants away from your corn crop.

Tip: don't plant dill or celery near your carrots as they release a substance that discourages growth.

grow

"In the spring, at the end of the day, you should smell like dirt."

MARGARET ATWOOD, *BLUEBEARD'S EGG*

Farro salad with spring greens

As the weather warms, the crops of spring – a verdant array including leafy greens, peas, broccoli and asparagus – begin to sprout. This salad uses vegetables at their freshest, raw or blanched to keep their flavor, and mixes them with crunchy grains and zesty vinaigrette.

SERVES 4

Salad

180 g (1 cup/6⅔ oz) cracked farro*

1 tablespoon sunflower oil

100 g (⅔ cup/3½ oz) peas, blanched

1 bunch asparagus, cut into 2 cm (⅘ in) pieces

150 g (1 cup/5¼ oz) fennel, shaved

60 g (½ cup/2 oz) pistachios, roughly chopped

2 spring onions, finely chopped

½ cup mint, finely sliced

¾ cup flat-leaf parsley, finely sliced

Dressing

2 tablespoons olive oil

juice and zest 1 lemon

1 teaspoon caster sugar

½ teaspoon ground cinnamon

100 g (⅔ cup/3½ oz) feta

This delicious salad can be customized to your vegetable garden bounty: green beans or broccolini can be used instead of asparagus, and edamame or broad beans instead of peas.

Salad

1. Rinse and drain farro. Put farro and enough water to cover it by 4 cm (2 in) in a medium-sized saucepan. Bring it to the boil over a high heat, then reduce heat to medium-low and simmer for about 12 minutes – the farro grains should be soft, but still have a bit of body. Drain and squeeze to remove excess water, then pat dry with paper towel.

2. Heat sunflower oil in a large frying pan over a medium-high heat. Add half the farro and cook, stirring, for about 5 minutes. Add half of the asparagus pieces, a squeeze of lemon juice, and cook for a further 3 minutes. Remove from the heat and set aside to cool.

3. Combine both cooked and uncooked batches of farro and asparagus, peas, fennel, pistachios, spring onions, mint and parsley in a large mixing bowl.

Dressing

1. Whisk together the olive oil, lemon zest and juice, cinnamon and sugar until sugar dissolves. Add dressing to the salad and toss gently until thoroughly combined. Crumble feta over to serve.

*There are a few different varieties of farro available, whole, cracked, pearled and semi-pearled. Cooking times vary. Other grains like quinoa, freekah and bourghal would also work well.

Raise plants from seed

Get your vegetables and herbs off to a great start by raising them from seed. Turn household waste and recyclables like eggshells, egg cartons, toilet paper rolls and folded newspaper into containers for your seedlings – and watch them grow into edible and ornamental delights.

GATHER EMPTY EGG CARTON / EGGSHELLS / NEEDLE AND SAFE HEAT SOURCE / QUALITY SEED-RAISING MIX / SEEDS OF YOUR CHOICE / NEWSPAPER / WATERING CAN / LABELS / PEN

Propagation is the process of creating new plants from seeds, cuttings, roots or bulbs. Seeds can be propagated, or 'raised' in a number of ways, including in items destined for the compost or recycling bin, like eggshells, egg cartons, toilet paper rolls and newspaper. Biodegradable containers like these are ideal for raising seeds in, as unlike the plastic trays you buy seedlings in at a plant nursery, they can be placed directly in the soil. This reduces 'transplant shock', and increases seedlings' chances of survival. Eggshells offer the added bonus of providing extra calcium for your plants and soil.

Preparing your seeds

1. Label your containers with the date and type of seeds you are planting, so that you can see how long it takes for your seeds to germinate.

2. If using egg cartons, simply place them on a waterproof tray. Before you start, make sure you provide drainage by holding a needle in the flame of a candle until it's hot, then carefully piercing a hole in the bottom of each eggshell. Toilet paper and newspaper rolls can be placed vertically and side by side in a dish with a decent lip, like a baking tray or pie dish.

3. Fill the containers with your seed-raising mix, gently pressing into each container. Plant one seed per container if the seeds are large (such as peas and beans), and a pinch of seeds if they are smaller (such as lettuce or rocket). Plant larger seeds deeper, and smaller seeds closer to the surface. Make sure your seeds are covered by a thin layer of seed-raising mix.

4. Place the containers in a light and protected location, but not in direct sunlight as this can burn delicate seedlings. Water gently – the soil should be kept moist but not saturated.

5. Your seedlings will initially produce two leaves called cotyledons, followed by the plant's true leaves. Once three to four true leaves have grown, it's time to plant out your seedlings. Gently take one container at a time and plant in your garden, just below the surface soil. Refer to the seed packet for advice on spacing, then give your newly planted seedlings a good soak, and enjoy watching them grow.

Compost

Composting is nature's way of turning kitchen scraps into 'black gold' that you can use to top up and supercharge your pot plants and garden beds. Composting recycles valuable nutrients and creates fresh soil packed with humus – a substance that is essential for healthy, fertile plant growth.

GATHER COMPOSTING RECEPTACLE OF YOUR CHOICE / MIXED VEGGIE SCRAPS / FRESH GRASS CLIPPINGS / DRIED LEAVES / LUCERNE OR PEA STRAW / MANURES / WOOD ASH OR GARDEN LIME / WORMS

When you make quality compost, you create humus; that marvellous colloidal substance that has 900% the water-holding capacity of sand, maintains soil structure, binds nutrients, balances soil pH and is essential for healthy, fertile plant growth.

Composting set-up

Decide what size and type of compost to create based on your budget and garden size. If you have a large garden you can use recycled wooden pallets, bricks, or straw bales for your base. You'll need a compost pile at least a metre square for best results. Plastic tubs that sit directly on your garden beds are suited to small spaces.

To deter rodents, use a fully enclosed bin, or place sturdy mesh beneath an open-bottomed bin. Take care that a fully enclosed composting bin does not overheat in summer and kill off your precious worms.

Which worms?

Worms help break down scraps by eating waste and excreting nutrients (castings). Indian blue, tiger and red worms are considered the best, as they eat the equivalent of their body weight in a day. Source a handful from a friend's compost or buy some at your local nursery.

A balanced diet

Maintaining the right carbon–nitrogen balance helps compost to break down quickly and reduces unwanted odours, pests and insects. Healthy compost should not smell bad.

Your food scraps will be high in nitrogen, so it's important to add carbon-rich materials such as pea straw, lucerne, dried leaves or dried grass on top each time you add scraps. In smaller compost bins, keep your worms happy by minimising citrus, onions and garlic, and chop scraps into smaller pieces so that they break down faster; larger composts will be balanced by other materials. Add handfuls of aged manure for extra nutrients and a sprinkling of wood ash or garden lime to help balance acidity.

Water, air and temperature

Your compost needs to be moist, but not saturated – like a wrung-out sponge. You can encourage organic matter to break down by adding materials in a range of sizes to create air pockets and airflow, and tumbling your compost with a gardening fork to mix your ingredients and aerate it. The right temperature is also important (between 55–75°C [130–165°F] is best). This is important for the health of your worms, especially in closed systems where the worms cannot burrow into deeper ground. Site your compost where it won't get too cold in winter, or overheat in summer. Smaller compost bins have a limited amount of material, which lowers the temperature and means everything takes longer to break down.

When is it ready?

Your compost is ready when it no longer has any odour other than a damp earthy aroma, is a uniform dark brown crumbly texture and is cool to the touch.

Keep chickens

There are more chickens in the world than any other species of bird, and they make for productive outdoor pets: they'll compost your food scraps, provide you with fresh organic eggs, and produce an ongoing supply of high-nitrogen fertilizer that is very good for your garden.

GATHER CHICKEN COOP AND RUN / CHICKENS OF YOUR CHOICE / PEA STRAW OR LUCERNE / LAYER PELLETS AND GRAINS / WATERER / VEGGIE SCRAPS

Like people, chickens need a balanced diet, fresh water, TLC, freedom to roam, and a cosy home (the 'coop') to come back to.

Before you decide to purchase chickens for your backyard, check your local authority's guidelines on how many you can keep and the recommended location of your chicken coop and run. Roosters can be gentlemanly, but noisy, and their crowing is often not allowed in urban neighborhoods.

How many?

A normal urban backyard has the capacity to keep 2–4 chickens, and a small number like this is ideal, as in the wild chickens live in small social groups. They also need plenty of room to scratch and dirt bathe, as this keeps them happy and helps to manage parasites. Chickens can turn your garden into a moonscape in a matter of hours, so make sure you limit numbers to what's manageable within your garden. Other considerations include the ongoing cost of feed and how many eggs you would like.

The coop and run

Next you need to work out what coop and run you would like. A chicken coop (or hen house) is a building where chickens are kept. A coop contains nest boxes for egg laying and a roost where the birds can perch and sleep. Dropping boards or another material, usually straw, go under the roost for catching poo and for ease of cleaning.

The run is an outdoor area attached to the coop where your chickens can safely roam. Your coop and run need to be fox-and-dog proof to keep your feathered friends safe and happy. There are many chicken coops available to purchase ready made, or you can build your own from a variety of salvaged and new materials.

Wormwood, tansy and lavender are herbs that repel insects, and can be strewn on the floor of your coop and run for additional hygiene. Pea straw and lucerne make great bedding material, and your garden or compost also benefit when it's time to clean the coop. Poo should be removed daily, and the entire coop cleaned out and freshened up every 2–3 weeks. A light mite dust or regular sprinkling of wood ash in the coop helps to keep parasites like mites and lice under control.

Which breeds?

There are hundreds of chicken breeds, but only around 20 that are recommended for domestic egg production purposes. It's a good idea to explore the varieties of chicken that are available in your area, and get advice on which ones are best for you to keep. Try visiting a city farm or poultry breeder, talking with neighbors who keep chickens, or consulting your local authority. ISA Browns and Rhode Island Reds are popular in Australia, Europe and the USA for their consistently reliable laying.

Bantam chickens are a smaller breed and are excellent for gardens with limited space. Their eggs are smaller but equally delicious, they require less food, and will also cause less damage to your garden when free roaming.

There is a world of ornate and gorgeous heirloom varieties to choose from – they may not give you as many eggs, but they'll delight you with their beautifully patterned feathers and unique personalities. Wyandottes, Aracaunas, Faverolles, Barnevelders – the list is extensive. Some chicken breeds are also naturally more broody (inclined to lay and incubate eggs) than others, which is great if you want to raise your own chickens. Just remember you're likely to get a batch of male and female chicks, so you'll need to think about what to do with all those budding roosters.

Get started by buying your chickens as 16–20 week-old point-of-lay pullets (a pullet is a young hen) from a reputable poultry breeder who has vaccinated them. This means they'll be less susceptible to poultry diseases and illnesses, and it also means you'll get to enjoy them as babies.

Be cautious about purchasing chickens from markets, as you may also unwittingly introduce sick birds into your flock.

Keeping your chickens healthy

Chickens can succumb to a number of pests and bacterial and viral diseases. Some, like Avian Pox, can be cured, while others like Fowl Cholera are incurable. Keep an eye out for changes to their poo, appetite, behaviour, feathers and skin. Anything untoward should be closely monitored, and if necessary, you should consult a vet or other chicken expert.

You can help prevent diseases through good hygiene and a varied diet. They enjoy a diet of mixed grains, layer pellets, fresh food scraps, insects, worms and fresh greens. Shell grit helps their digestion and gives them an extra source of calcium for ongoing egg production. You can purchase layer pellets and grains from pet food and stockfeed stores.

Feeding your chickens greens makes their egg yolks yellower and provides them with extra protein. It's also important to make sure your chickens have an unlimited supply of fresh, cool and clean drinking water – ideally being served in a waterer that will supply clean water on demand. Adding fresh garlic to their drinking water every few months is a natural worming treatment, and you can also use a commercial worming liquid available from stockfeed stores.

Introducing new birds to the pecking order

Chickens are notorious for their pecking order antics. As social creatures, they are quick to establish a hierarchy, and they do this by pecking each other. Regardless of whether you keep only one breed of chickens, or several, there will be a dominant character or two who assert themselves over more sensitive birds. You can deliberately choose breeds that are more docile such as Silky, Australorp, Cochin and Brahma, however some will be more aggressive than others; it's just in their nature. When introducing new chickens to your flock, make sure you include at least two at a time for easier assimilation into your hen harem. Fence the new birds in a separate area next to the main coop and run for a week, then introduce them into the coop at night, and cross your fingers that they all wake up friends in the morning.

Hail the honeybee

Bees are extraordinary. Experts estimate that it takes 10 million foraging trips to make the equivalent of one jar of honey. Here are some ways to get more honeybee love in your life. In the process, you'll help to keep bee populations and the plants they serve healthy and diverse.

A single honeybee colony can contain between 10,000 and 60,000 bees. In a single day, a worker bee might visit more than 500 flowers foraging for nectar and pollen. Bees love nectar, the sugar and carbohydrate-filled liquid produced in flowers.

Of course, bees don't collect nectar to feed us – they collect it to feed adult bees. It's passed from foraging worker bees to worker house bees, then deposited into honeycomb cells. The house bees fan the nectar until enough of the water content evaporates and it turns into honey, then they cap it with wax. The honey provides the bees with a winter food source to dip into when they are unable to forage outside for food.

Left to their own devices, bees make enough honey to feed their entire colony through winter. But with the right kind of love and attention, a colony can be coaxed into producing more honey than they really need, which provides us with delicious honey for eating, and with beeswax for making candles and waxes, and nourishing skin creams and conditioners. Raw, untreated honey can also be used medicinally to treat sore throats and help to heal wounds.

Bees also play a vital role as pollinators. This means that they transport pollen from male to female flowers, enabling plants to grow fruits and vegetables and to reproduce.

Buy local honey

Connecting with local apiarists (beekeepers) is a great way to connect with local bees.

Many small-scale beekeepers sell or share their honey with their local community, so begin by talking with your local garden centre and researching beekeeping groups and associations to find out what's happening in your neighborhood or town.

Beekeepers harvest honey from their hives in mid to late summer, after the bees have made the most of the nectar available from flowering plants.

A bee can travel more than 6.5 km (4 mi) in search of nectar in one day, so when you're tasting local honey, you're tasting honey made from the nectar of flowers in a 10 km (6 mi) radius of the hive location. Who knows, perhaps you're tasting honey made from the nectar of flowers in your own garden.

Grow a bee-friendly garden

Planting flowers and herbs rich in nectar is a sure-fire way to attract bees to your garden or outdoor space. You'll have a beautiful, colorful garden to enjoy – and a productive one, too.

Bees favour flowers that are yellow, purple or blue, so plant forget-me-nots, lavender, catmint, salvia, phacelia and nasturtiums. Bee-friendly herbs include basil, thyme, sage, rocket, borage, chives, garlic chives and cilantro.

Keep bees

There are many types of bees, but the busiest, and therefore the most popular for honey production, is the European honeybee (*Apis mellifera*).

Before you get started, contact the relevant local authority to find out their policy for beekeeping. Some don't allow beekeeping in urban environments, while others set limits on hive numbers according to the size of a garden, or require you to obtain a beekeeping licence.

Once you've done all the necessary research, you'll need to gather tools from a local supplier, including an extractor, protective equipment, a hive and most importantly, a nucleus colony (a small honey bee colony created from a larger colony) with a queen and worker bees.

Next, you'll need to learn how to look after your hives. Practical skills like these are best learned in the field, so attending an introductory course at your local beekeeping association is a great idea. You'll learn things like how to handle bees safely, where best to locate your hive, how often to inspect it, how to keep a hive healthy and identify disease, and how to harvest honey. You'll also learn fascinating details, like why beekeepers wear white (one theory is that bees have an ancient memory that black bears are robbers), and when it's best not to disturb them, because they'll almost always respond angrily (on a cold morning, or after rain).

It's a nice courtesy to let immediate neighbors know, as they might notice increased activity at sunrise and sunset when the bees leave and return to the hive.

Host hives

If you're not quite ready to keep your own bees, hosting a hive is a great option.

Bees form new colonies (this is called swarming) in spring, when the hive population is growing and a new queen bee is born. The old queen departs, leaving the remaining bees and her home to the new queen and her expanding colony.

Beekeepers often need new places to house their old queen and her loyal bees at this time, so if you have a space that is suited to bees – that's one with a consistent and accessible supply of water, and one that's reliably well drained, and away from draughts – consider hosting. Sunshine is important too, as it warms the hive and motivates the bees to start working.

Hosting space is often exchanged for a honey tax – and if your visiting apiarist is willing, you'll be able to watch and learn and perhaps even participate.

Sprout seeds and beans

Sprouting your own edible seeds and beans is a sweet, simple and extremely satisfying way to do some small-scale, edible indoor gardening that is very good for you. What's more, sprouts are the baby animals of the plant world; they're tiny and cute and if you give them love, they'll love you right back.

GATHER TABLESPOON / DRIED SEEDS OR BEANS / MASON JARS / SCISSORS / CHEESECLOTH / RUBBER BANDS

A 'sprout' is the tiny, first shoot of a plant to emerge from its seed or bean, while 'sprouting' is the practice of germination: starting the growing process by encouraging the first sprout of the plant to unfurl and emerge from its shell.

Benefits of sprouting

When you eat sprouts, you're eating a living food packed full of enzymes, vitamins and nutrients. And when you sprout, you're creating a delicious, economical highly nutritious food source for yourself. Sprouts are at their most nutritious (and tasty) eaten raw. They can be added to salads and smoothies, sprinkled on toast (try them with avocado or hummus) or simply eaten on their own.

Sourcing seeds and beans for sprouting

When choosing seeds to sprout, make sure you purchase seeds intended for sprouting (versus planting), to ensure they are suitable for eating.

Your local health food store, grocery store or supermarket should stock at least some of the seeds or beans that are suitable for sprouting. Some of the more popular varieties are alfalfa, buckwheat, chickpea, lentil, mung bean, quinoa, radish, red cabbage and soybean.

Jar sprouting method

There are a number of different sprouting methods. Jar sprouting is the easiest to get started with, and gives you a hands-on appreciation for the simple wonders of sprouting.

You should sprout just one type of seed in a jar. This is because each variety takes a different amount of time to sprout, usually from 3–7 days.

1. Start by placing a few tablespoons of your chosen seeds in a clean jar and cover them with approximately 5 cm (2 in) of lukewarm water.

2. Cover the opening of the jar with a round of cheesecloth cut to size (with an inch or so spare), secure it with a rubber band or mason jar lid, and let it sit overnight.

3. The next day, drain the water out of the jar by securing the excess cheesecloth with your fingers, holding the jar over your kitchen sink, and giving it a gentle shake.

4. Next, rinse the seeds by adding fresh water to the jar through the cheesecloth and swirling the seeds around, then draining the jar over the sink again.

5. Put the jar in a warm, dark place and repeat the washing and draining process daily to avoid mould and encourage germination. Continue until your sprouts are still fairly small and just starting to turn green; usually 3–5 days.

6. Store your sprouts in a covered bowl or food storage bag with a paper towel inside to absorb excess moisture, and eat them within a week.

walk in nature

"Walking ... is how the body measures itself against the earth."

REBECCA SOLNIT, *WANDERLUST: A HISTORY OF WALKING*

Energy balls

These little snacks are moist and soft, with sweet and nutty flavors. They are perfect to tuck into your lunchbox to keep you going on a spring walk, to eat as a quick breakfast, or for a pick-me-up treat. And there's nothing more to them than blending the ingredients together and shaping them into balls.

EACH RECIPE MAKES 10-16 BALLS, DEPENDING ON SIZE

Fig and pistachio energy balls

100 g (1 cup/3½ oz) rolled oats

100 g (½ cup/3½ oz) dried figs

90 g (¾ cup/3 oz) sultanas

60 g (½ cup/2 oz) pistachios

½ teaspoon cinnamon

1 teaspoon vanilla extract

60 ml (¼ cup/2 fl oz) tahini

2 tablespoons apple juice

1 tablespoon olive oil

1 tablespoon sesame seeds

¼ teaspoon salt

Cocoa, chia and coconut energy balls

100 g (1 cup/4 oz) almond meal

30 g (¼ cup/1 oz) raw cocoa powder

30 g (¼ cup/1 oz) maca powder

185 g (1 cup/6½ oz) medijool dates, seeds removed and roughly chopped

2 tablespoons chia seeds

1 teaspoon vanilla extract

2 teaspoons maple syrup

3 tablespoons coconut oil, melted

¼ teaspoon salt

These balls are packed with protein and good fats from the variety of seeds and nuts providing slow-releasing energy to keep you nourished and full, as well as giving you an instant boost from the nutrients and natural sugars in the dried fruit.

Method (works for both recipes)

1. Combine all ingredients in a food processor and blend until finely chopped and well combined. You can blend a little more or less depending on whether you prefer a smoother or chunkier texture. The finer the mixture, the easier they will be to bind. If you prefer a chunky texture, blend half of the mixture until very fine, then leave the other half more chunky and combine the two.

2. Once blended, squeeze together small handfuls of the mixture to make tightly packed balls about 3 cm (1 in) in diameter. You can dust the fig balls with a little cinnamon or roll them in sesame seeds, and the chocolate balls you can dust with cocoa or roll in coconut.

3. Transfer balls to an airtight container and keep in the refrigerator for up to a week.

Weave a wreath of wildflowers

Celebrate spring and its explosion of life and color by getting out into the wilds and foraging for flowers to weave into a wreath. Wildflower wreaths can be placed in the centre of dining tables, hung from windows and doors, or even worn as crowns. They also make great seasonal gifts for nature-loving friends.

GATHER WILDFLOWERS / SCISSORS / RAFFIA OR TWINE

Wildflowers are flowers that grow in the wild – and they've always been that way. They have not been intentionally seeded or planted, but perhaps carried as seeds by the wind, or a bird, then nurtured into full, glorious flowers by the right combination of sun and rain.

The term 'wildflower' can refer to a flowering plant as a whole – not just the flower, and even when it's not in bloom. Many countries have elected a native wildflower as their national flower – a national flag of the plant world, if you will. England's is the rose, Hungary's is the tulip, Mexico's is the dahlia, and Scotland's is the thistle. And while the non-native rose is the floral emblem of the United States as a whole, each state has its own 'state flower', often native, like Connecticut's mountain laurel, Arizona's saguaro cactus blossom, and Colorado's Rocky Mountain columbine. The national flower of Australia is the golden wattle, Sturt's desert rose is the Northern Territory's state flower, and pink heath is Victoria's.

Gathering your wildflowers

Wildflowers grow where nature is allowed to have its way: in parks, on grass verges, alongside rivers, up hills and mountains.

Look for flower stems that are flexible and bendy, and bear in mind flowers that drop a lot of pollen are going to continue to do that once you've woven them into a wreath. Take care to pick just the flower, not the roots and to leave some flowers on each plant cluster for pollinators like bees to visit, so that the plant survives to flower in future seasons.

Making your wreath

Begin by cutting or gently breaking the stems of the flowers until they are much the same length.

Take two flowers. Loop the first stem around the second stem. Gently pinch the bottoms of both stems together and pull them down, to tighten the bind. Then take another flower, place it half way down the looped stems you've already made, loop it around and tighten it. Carry on in this way, slowly but surely wrapping and weaving flowers and stems together, until you have a braided length that is long enough for your purpose.

To close your wreath, wrap (or braid) the two ends together until it holds its form. You can also wrap a piece of vine, ivy, raffia or twine around the whole wreath to make it more secure.

Keeping it fresh

How long your wreath remains fresh will depend on the type of flowers you use; most last a day or two. You can help by spraying the wreath with water, and hanging it upside down so the flower heads face down overnight.

Note: It's not always legal to pick wildflowers, so make sure to check local regulations.

Make a pocket press

Nature is an abundant gifter at any time of year, but especially so in spring, when flowers start to bloom. This nature press is made for your pocket, so you can carry it with you whenever you go somewhere wild. Collect colorful flowers and place them into your nature press as spring mementos.

GATHER PLYWOOD / CORRUGATED CARDBOARD / BLOTTING PAPER / TWO STRAPS / FOUR D RINGS / PENCIL / RULER / SCISSORS / NEEDLE AND THREAD OR SEWING MACHINE / CRAFT GLUE

This pocket nature press is made up of layers of corrugated cardboard and blotting paper sandwiched between two pieces of plywood secured with a strap.

Each layer of cardboard and blotting paper gives you a spot to place a flower or leaf – the project allows for five layers, but you can make it as big as you want.

Method

1. Start by cutting the plywood (or get your local hardware store to cut it) into two equal-sized pieces that will fit into the pocket you're most likely to keep your press in (most pockets measure about 9 x 6.5 cm [4 x 3 in]).

2. Take a piece of sandpaper and gently work the corners and edges of the plywood, so that it feels soft and smooth in the palm of your hand.

3. Cut six pieces of corrugated cardboard to the same size as the plywood covers (corrugated cardboard is commonly used for packaging, so try to recycle).

4. Cut five pieces of blotting paper the same length as your cardboard and plywood, but twice the width. For example, if your cover measures 9 x 6.5 cm (4 x 3 in), cut each piece of paper to measure 9 x 13 cm (4 x 6 in). You can also use plain newsprint, tissue paper, or even printing paper.

5. Fold each piece of paper in half, so all are the same size as the cardboard. Then, trim the corners so that they too are rounded.

6. Now you're ready to layer your press. Start by placing one of the plywood covers on a stable surface, then a piece of cardboard, then a piece of blotting paper, then another piece of cardboard, then another piece of blotting paper, making sure you align the folded sides of the paper. Carry on alternating the paper and cardboard, then place the second piece of wood on top.

7. Sew an end of one strap (you can source straps from a craft shop) around two metal D rings (a metal loop shaped like a D, available from craft shops). You can do this by hand, or on a sewing machine. Repeat with the other strap.

8. The straps will hold the press together. Place a strap's two D rings on the front of your press near the bottom of the plywood and wrap the attached strap around the entire press. Weave the end of the strap through the two D rings. Glue the strap to the back of the nature press to make it secure. Repeat with your other strap near the top of the press.

9. Let it dry thoroughly.

Happy pressing!

Make a swing

Humans have been enjoying swinging back and forth through the air since, forever. Have you seen a beautiful tree, lush garden setting or stunning view that could be made even lovelier with the simple pleasure of a swing? You're never too old to enjoy soaring high, with the wind at your heels.

GATHER WOOD / POLY TWIST ROPE / HANDSAW / SANDPAPER / DRILL

Your swing is going to hold precious cargo (that's you!) and built right, it will last for generations, so take your time with this project.

Choose your materials

Source a strong, durable plank of wood that is at least 2.5 cm (1 in) thick. Never use pine, or wood that has already been used and is split, splintered or water-soaked. It's too weak.

Poly twist rope is the best for your swing, as it is durable, won't break for a million years, and gives good grip.

Choose your location

Choose a thick, living limb growing parallel to the ground for your swing.

Make your swing

If the wood is not the right size already, cut a board measuring 45 x 25 cm (18 x 10 in) (or your hardware store can do this for you). Use the sandpaper to smooth the top and edges, so you don't get splinters.

Drill four holes a little bigger than the thickness of your rope in each of the four corners of the wood. Space them about 2.5 cm (1 in) in from the corners of the wood, and try to make them as even as possible.

Next, cut your rope. You'll need two lengths of rope that are twice the projected height of the swing plus 3.5 m (138 in). Make sure you cut a little more than you need – if you cut it too short, you'll have to start over, but you can always trim it.

Hang your swing

This stage will be easier if you have someone helping you, so involve a friend.

Take one of the pieces of rope and double it over so that the two cut ends are together.

Carefully climb a ladder (or just climb the tree) to the branch you're going to suspend the swing from, taking your rope with you.

Holding on to the looped end, place the rope over the branch then thread the two cut ends through the loop. Tug the two cut ends to secure the loop against the tree branch then repeat this process with the second piece of rope. Place it the same distance apart on the branch as the holes are on the seat.

Now you're ready to thread the four lengths of rope through the four holes you drilled in the swing. Adjust it to the right height. Your feet should hang just a little bit off the ground.

Finally, secure the ropes in place by tying each of the lengths in a figure eight stopper knot (see page 195) underneath the swing. Then ready, get set, go.

watch the sunrise

"I felt my lungs inflate with the onrush of
scenery – air, mountains, trees, people. I thought,
'This is what it is to be happy.'"

— SYLVIA PLATH, *THE BELL JAR*

Find a sit spot

A sit spot is a place somewhere out of doors – perhaps a well-shaped rock, a pretty corner in your garden, or a comfortable park bench – that you go to often and regularly, to sit. While you're sitting, open your senses. Look, listen, feel, smell, and even taste the natural world as it unfolds all around you. Let it fill you, then go about your day.

Finding your own sit spot and visiting it to sit in quiet, absorbent contemplation of the seasons, day in and day out, is a wonderful and grounding way to be calmed, delighted and refreshed by nature.

Finding a sit spot

The perfect sit spot has five simple qualities:

1. It is close to your work or home; no more than two minutes from your door. This way you can get to it quickly and spontaneously and you're more likely to maintain a sit spot practice.

2. It is close to nature. It doesn't have to be a lot of nature. You might live in an apartment building and create a sit spot on your verandah, or make a resolve to spend more time in the park across the road from where you get your morning coffee.

3. You can lose yourself being alone there. It's important to be able to expand your senses and let go of your thinking to really let nature in.

4. It is safe. You need to be able to relax and shift your focus away from yourself. This will be hard to do if you need to be vigilant about your safety, so pick a spot where you know you'll be able to be at ease.

5. It has you in it. There's no such thing as a perfect sit spot; it's simply a matter of finding one that inspires or relaxes you. It's okay to have more than one sit spot, or to move onto a different sit spot when you feel like it.

Tips for sitting

When you're in your spot, close your eyes and breathe deeply. Then open your eyes and look around you. What do you see? What's different from the last time you sat here? What's the same? Listen to the sounds around you. Do you hear birds? What else do you hear? What can you feel on your skin, or smell on the breeze? What can you taste on your tongue?

Try to go to your sit spot at the same time every day. Then change times. What stays the same? What is different? How do you feel in your space at different times of day?

Keeping a journal

Some people like to write or draw in a sit spot journal. If you do this, let your mind wander into nature then back to the page. Don't think too much about what you're writing or drawing; try to get into a free-flowing state, and let nature take you by surprise.

Mix seed bombs

Making seed bombs and throwing, concealing, digging, or just gently placing them in places you see that could use a little love - think vacant lots, and random patches of public dirt - is a fun and productive way to get your hands dirty, and adds a little (or a lot) of beauty to your world.

GATHER CLAY / NATIVE SEEDS / COMPOST OR POTTING MIX / WATER

Seed bombs were created by members of the guerrilla gardening movement: green-thumbed city dwellers, all over the world, who have been taking it upon themselves to beautify neglected plots of land since the 1970s.

Seed bombs are simple constructions of clay, water, compost or potting mix (or even worm castings), and native seeds. They're relatively cheap to make, and make for a fun afternoon project. See page 157 for tips on how to find and dig for clay.

The seeds of native flowers and plants are the most desirable for seed bombing, as they will grow well without a lot of tending. They also won't crowd out other plants, disrupt bird and insect populations, or do other environmental damage.

Method

1. Lay your clay, seeds (a mixture of seeds, or just one type) and compost out on a surface that you don't mind getting a little dirty.

2. Divide them into five parts clay; one part compost (or potting mix); and one part seeds.

3. Next, form the compound for the outside of the seed bombs by combining the clay and the compost. The clay might be quite tough until you've warmed it with your hands, so don't be afraid to get stuck in. Adding a drop or two of water can help to make it more pliable, but be careful not to overdo it. The mixture should be malleable, but not too sloppy. Carefully add more water if you need to, one drop at a time, and rub it all together until it has a gritty, dough-like mixture.

4. Add the seeds and gradually work them in, using the same rubbing and kneading method.

5. Tear the mixture into pieces about the size of a nectarine, and roll them into balls.

6. You can plant your seed bombs while they are moist or let them dry. As long as they are watered once they're planted – either by you, or by the rain – the clay will break down, and the seeds will grow.

In a few weeks' time, you should see your seeds starting to grow into beautiful plants and flowers for the whole community to enjoy.

Disclaimer: Seed bombing can be a legal grey area. Check with your local authority for guidelines regarding seed bombing.

climb a tree

—

"In short, all good things are wild and free."

— HENRY DAVID THOREAU, WALKING

Forage and create a wall hanging

On any ramble in the woods, you might find a black feather, a stick with twists and turns, a leaf that an insect has nibbled into a polka-dot pattern. These found objects can find their way onto the wall of your home in a forage hanging that will remind you of natural world explorations past and present ...

GATHER STICKS / FEATHERS / SEED PODS / SCISSORS / COLORED THREAD / HOT GLUE GUN

You only have to think of the tiny Adelie penguin who carefully selects the biggest and best-looking rocks from the wilds of Antarctica to make his nest to realize that selecting objects to make our homes more attractive is a common trait across the animal kingdom. But you don't have to shell out money to liven up your house; simply step outside into the natural world and you'll be enchanted to discover the array of bits and bobs that can be turned into a naturally beautiful wall hanging.

Method

1. Take your string bag (see page 213) and head out into the great outdoors. Who knows what you'll find? From a twig that has dropped off a tree, to a shell long abandoned by its owner, the natural world has an abundance of materials no longer used by their original owners just waiting to be picked up by ... well, you!

2. Items with small holes in them are ideal. Otherwise you'll need objects light enough to be held up by knotted yarn. Of course, if you're handy with scissors or a drill, you can simply create a small hole in your found object yourself. Be careful – you don't want to damage the integrity of your item.

3. Grab the colored thread and either tie it in a knot near the top of one of your foraged items or knot the thread through the small hole. Once you've secured your item, begin looping the thread around your object. You can use as many colors as you like and wrap it however you choose. These loops aren't structural – they are to pretty up your nest.

4. If you have a glue gun, use it to make the ends secure. Otherwise you'll need to make sure your knots are tight.

5. Lay your wrapped items in front of you and arrange in an order you would like them to hang. Use sticks as the structure of your wall hanging – they are strong enough to hold everything else up. Using another thread of your choice, loop one end around one object and knot it, and then tie the other end around the item you want to hang off the first object. Remember to double knot your ends to secure all of your threads.

SUMMER

walk barefoot

"Adopt the pace of nature: her secret is patience."

— RALPH WALDO EMERSON

look up

———

CIRROCUMULUS / HIGH CLOUD

WHITE, STREAKY CLOUDS, OFTEN GROUPED IN BEAUTIFUL PATTERNS.
INDICATE FAIR WEATHER IN MOST CLIMATES; IN THE TROPICS, CAN MEAN
A STORM OR HURRICANE IS COMING.

ALTOCUMULUS / MIDDLE CLOUD

FLUFFY, GREYISH-WHITE CLOUDS WITH A LOT OF CONTRAST BETWEEN LIGHT AND DARK.
IF YOU SEE THEM IN THE MORNING, PREPARE FOR RAIN IN THE AFTERNOON.

STRATOCUMULUS / LOW CLOUD

PATCHES OF FLUFFY WHITE OR GREY CLOUDS, CLOSE OVERHEAD.
THEY DON'T INDICATE RAIN, BUT IT'S GOING TO BE A CLOUDY DAY.

STRATUS / LOW CLOUD

SOLID GREY CLOUDS THAT LOOK LIKE (AND OFTEN ARE) AN ELEVATED FOG.
INDICATE DRIZZLE, RAIN AND EVEN LIGHT SNOW.

Read the clouds

In the past, people looked to the sky and drew on their knowledge of cloud types to predict, understand and prepare for the weather. By schooling yourself in the basics of meteorology and weather lore, you too can read the clouds, and accurately forecast the weather.

Weather lore

You've probably heard the old saying, 'Red sky at night, shepherd's delight. Red sky in morning, shepherd's warning'.

This pretty rhyme is an example of weather lore; a centuries-old collection of sayings, rhymes and proverbs that people used as memory aids to help them recognize and prepare for what the changing skies might bring.

Weather lore often contains agricultural or maritime language and symbolism as many sayings were developed by farmers, shepherds and sailors, whose livelihoods depended on them being able to accurately predict the weather.

Here are some of the better known weather proverbs explained to get you started.

Red sky at night, shepherd's delight

In many countries, weather systems come from the west, and the sun sets in the western sky. If the sky is red at night, the setting sun is illuminating clear skies in the west, where the next day's weather is coming from.

Red sky in morning, shepherd's warning

This is an accurate predictor of bad weather ahead as the appearance of a red sky in the east means a spell of good weather has already passed, most likely making way for a wet and windy low pressure system.

Mare's tails and mackerel scales make tall ships bring in their sails

The wispy, candy floss–like clouds that form the mare's tails in this evocative saying are called cirrus clouds. When cirrus clouds visit a blue sky and are followed by transparent, sheet-like cirrostratus clouds – the mackerel scales – it's a sign that pressure is building up. The clouds are most likely leading a warm front, and warm fronts bring lots of rain.

This is also where the term 'mackerel sky' comes from, as the patterns made by cirrostratus clouds resemble the scales of the mackerel.

When halo rings moon or sun, rain's approaching on the run

When a ring, or halo, appears around the moon or sun, it's likely that rain is not far away. The halo is caused by ice crystals forming in high clouds, which refract the light from the moon or sun. As the ice crystals travel lower, precipitation (wet weather) becomes more likely.

Whether you enjoy rhymes or not, one thing is certain: bad weather never arrives without a few warning signs in the clouds first. And once you know what you're looking for, the coming changes are easy to spot.

Describing and understanding clouds

Clouds can be recognized and understood by their shape, and their height in the sky.

Cloud shapes

There are four basic cloud shapes:

• Cirrus clouds are thin and feathery. The name comes from the Latin for 'curl' or 'fringe'.

• Cumulus clouds are fluffy and seem to sit on top of one another. The name comes from the Latin for 'heap' or 'pile'.

• Nimbus clouds are murky rain clouds. The name comes from the Latin for 'rain'.

• Stratus clouds are long, streaky and blanket-like. The name comes from the Latin for 'layer'.

The remaining cloud types are either combinations of the basic four listed above (such as cirrostratus, cirrocumulus, stratocumulus, nimbostratus, cumulonimbus), or preceded by 'alto'. Alto comes from the Latin 'altus', meaning high. This is somewhat misleading, as altostratus and altocumulus are more likely to be middle clouds.

High clouds – cirrus, cirrostratus, cirrocumulus

High clouds sit more than 3 miles above ground level. You'll see them at the top of a high mountain, or from an aeroplane. They're made of ice crystals, not water, which means they won't rain on you. They sit so high in the sky that they don't block sunlight, either.

Cirrus and cirrocumulus are particularly lovely fair weather clouds, but they can indicate that a change is on the way. Keep an eye on their movement, and on the direction in which cirrus's feathery wisps are pointing so you can work out what direction the weather front is moving in.

Cirrostratus tend to cover the whole sky, and are a more definite indicator that wet weather is on the way.

Middle clouds – altostratus, altocumulus

Middle clouds sit between 1 to 4 miles above ground level. They are higher (well, mid-level) versions of low-hanging stratus or vertically mobile cumulus clouds. They are made of water and, if it's cold enough, ice. Both can block the sunlight, and indicate that rain is afoot.

Altocumulus clouds are often arranged in stunning patterns; if you see them in the morning, prepare for rain in the afternoon. Altostratus are high, sheet-like clouds that indicate stormy weather in the near future.

Low clouds – nimbus, stratus, stratocumulus, nimbostratus

Low clouds sit up to 1 mile above ground level. They often feel very close overhead, and usually block out sunlight.

Stratus clouds can bring fog, drizzle and light snow. Stratocumulus are just hanging about – they don't bring rain. Grey and murky nimbostratus are your standard rainclouds – if you see them, it's probably already raining.

Clouds with vertical mobility and growth – cumulus, cumulonimbus

Cumulus and cumulonimbus clouds have a low-hanging base and can grow dramatically upwards. When they remain low in the sky the weather will remain fair; vertical growth indicates bad weather like rain, lightning, hail and even tornadoes.

How to read the clouds

The best time to practise your cloud reading is following a spell of good weather. This is because it's much easier to forecast when the weather is turning bad.

Keep an eye on the direction clouds are moving or pointing, as this is a good indicator of the direction the weather is coming from and moving in.

Writing and sketching your observations and conclusions in a weather journal is a lovely way to practise the art of weather forecasting.

CIRRUS / HIGH CLOUD

WHITE AND WISPY CLOUDS THAT STRETCH ACROSS THE SKY.
INDICATE FAIR WEATHER NOW, POSSIBILITY OF CHANGE COMING.

CIRROSTRATUS / HIGH CLOUD

TRANSPARENT, SHEET-LIKE CLOUDS THAT COVER THE WHOLE SKY.
INDICATE DAMP WEATHER IS COMING IN THE NEXT 12-24 HOURS.

ALTOSTRATUS / MIDDLE CLOUD

GREYISH-WHITE CLOUDS THAT BLANKET ALL OR MOST OF THE SKY.
INDICATE STORMY WEATHER IN THE NEAR FUTURE.

NIMBOSTRATUS / LOW CLOUD

LARGE, FLAT SHEETS OF GREY CLOUD.
IF YOU SEE THESE, IT'S PROBABLY ALREADY RAINING.

Permaculture

Permaculture describes consciously designed landscapes and integrated living systems that support sustainable agriculture, buildings and settlements. It embraces patterns and relationships found in nature, and is guided by the principles of care for the earth, care for people, and sharing surplus.

The term permaculture was developed by Australians Bill Mollison and David Holmgren in the mid 1970s. Permaculture embraces patterns and relationships found in nature, the wisdom inherent in traditional societies, and a vision of sustainable agriculture and culture.

It's a framework for a holistic and sustainable life. You can take the journey in small and manageable steps as outlined below. Expertise is not required, but an open, curious and hands-on approach will set you on the path to a life of productivity, in sync with nature.

Care for the earth

Gardens are a wonderful way for you to physically care for the earth. You can grow a range of fresh organic produce for your needs and plant a variety of indigenous plants to provide habitat for local animals, birds and insects. Make good use of your natural resources through composting, capturing rainwater, saving seeds or harvesting timber. If your gardening space is small or limited, you can grow basic herbs, keep a worm farm, support your local organic farmers and markets by purchasing the fruits of their labor, or join your local community garden.

Ride a bike or take public transport instead of the car, or get involved with your local community planting group to restore a beloved piece of your neighborhood.

Care for people

Look after and nourish yourself, your families, relationships and world community. Be mindful of using your share of resources wisely, ensuring there is enough for all. Build interdependent relationships through shared activities – you can't do it all alone, and it's simply not as enjoyable! Take time out to be in nature and restore yourself. As you tune into nature's seasons, become more aware of your own internal rhythms and the overlap between them.

Share of surplus

When you have more than enough, gift your abundant seasonal produce, your time, tools, knowledge, talents and skills to create healthy, edible gardens, and sustainable homes and neighborhoods. It's about swapping and bartering, whether you're a gardener, musician, lawyer or baker – whatever your area of love and expertise.

Applying permaculture design to your garden

Permaculture principles are meant to help you design your garden and home to use energy and resources as wisely and elegantly as possible. Think about what you most want to include in your sustainable living space, and use a common sense approach to work out the best location for all the elements in your integrated home and garden.

Observe seasonal changes

Take the time to observe the relationships and patterns of nature in your garden, to better understand how you can enhance them for increased yields, and less work. What plants grow best where and with what other companion species? Which deciduous trees or vines do you plant to provide summer shade for your home and let the winter light in? Watch where the sun reaches into your garden across the seasons, where it gets windy or where there is protection from frost and snow.

Create a plan

Think about what you'd really like in your garden, and make a wishlist of your priorities. What do you enjoy eating that grows well in your area? Do you want to keep chickens (see page 19) or bees (see page 23)? Have you got room for a rainwater tank or compost (see page 17)? What trees, flowers, exotic or native species do you enjoy? Would you like an outdoor eating area? Play space for children? This helps you to see if you have enough room available for all the things you'd like. It's also important to think about what you can manage on an ongoing basis – remember you can build your dream garden slowly.

Map the relationships between various elements in your garden to maximize beneficial outcomes, for example your garage shed captures rainwater and provides a trellis for growing vines whilst providing shelter for your citrus trees. Think about what you visit frequently, and place those things closer to hand – kitchen herbs, your compost, annual vegetables.

If you don't feel comfortable drawing up your own garden plan, there are a number of permaculture practitioners and gardeners who can help.

Adapt

With all the best planning efforts, some things don't grow as well as expected. You just can't grow healthy cucumbers but your cilantro is consistently fabulous. Or you thought you'd really enjoy persimmons when you actually devour bucket loads of pears. Seek advice from neighbors, friendly gardeners, books or online forums, but don't be afraid to make changes either. Go with the flow, and enjoy experimenting with new things and just see what happens.

Take a permaculture course

One of the best ways to find out more about the wonderful world of permaculture in a hands-on way is to take a course. There's a range of different courses available to suit both urban and rural dwellers. One thing's for sure, your life will never be the same – in the best possible way.

Grow herbs

Herbs have been transported and traded all around the world, and were highly prized in earlier civilizations. Which makes it such a treat that these 'commodities' are so easy to grow and enjoy in pots or garden beds. Thyme, basil, mint – all will make fetching additions to your kitchen garden.

GATHER HERB SEEDS OR SEEDLINGS OF YOUR CHOICE / TROWEL / WATERING CAN

Herbs refer to the leafy green parts of a plant and can usually be used either fresh or dried, for food, flavoring, medicine, or perfume.

Herbs used for flavoring food are termed culinary herbs, and most are either perennials or annuals. Perennial herbs live for more than two years, and include chives, hyssop, lavender, lemon balm, lovage, marjoram, mint, oregano, rosemary, sage and thyme. Annuals complete their cycle of growth from seed to seed within one year, and include aloe vera, arugula, basil, borage, calendula, cayenne, chamomile, chervil, cilantro, dill, garlic and savory. A few herbs, like caraway, foxglove and parsley, are biennials, meaning it takes two years for them to complete their life cycle.

How to grow herbs

It's easy to grow leafy herbs from seeds or seedlings sourced from green-thumbed friends, markets and nurseries.

1. Find the right spot in your garden. You'll need to consider how much sun and moisture your herbs require – for example, Mediterranean herbs like sage, thyme, oregano and marjoram thrive in hot, dry conditions, whereas cilantro and parsley should be kept in semi-shade to enhance the growth of soft, tender leaves and preserve moisture. Cilantro is best sown in spring or fall in hotter climates, as it tends to bolt in summer – wanting to flower and produce seeds – while basil needs summer sun and enough water for it to flourish.

2. Most herb seeds are quite small. Plant these just below the surface of good quality garden soil and gently water them. Keep your seeds moist, especially when they are just sprouting or tender seedlings – but don't drown them.

3. For herb seedlings, dig a hole with your hand slightly bigger than the size of your plant, put the plant in and gently backfill your soil around the plant. Give it a good soak.

4. Keep tending your herbs, making sure they receive adequate water in their early stages of growth – even those that will eventually prefer much drier soil.

5. Harvest and enjoy your herbs regularly. When your annual or biennial herbs go to seed, you can let them naturally self-sow in the garden, or save the seeds once they've dried on the plant for the next season's growth.

6. Using your propagating skills (see page 183), keep your perennial herbs flourishing by simply separating a piece of the parent plant with roots intact to propagate another plant. Think about how perennials will fit into your overall garden design, as they'll be there for several years.

Make herbal teas

Herbal teas are also called tisanes, and are made by infusing or decocting plant materials, and sometimes herbs and spices, in hot water. Create your own brews to be enjoyed hot, cold, or somewhere in-between, and watch your plants unfurl their flavors.

GATHER HERBS OF YOUR CHOICE / KETTLE AND WATER / TEAPOT AND CUPS / HONEY AND LEMON TO TASTE

Herbal teas are distinct from black and green teas as they are not caffeinated, and are enjoyed the world over. In Morocco, mint tea is drunk with handfuls of fresh mint and generous helpings of sugar. In Turkey, apple tea is popular for its sweetness and refreshing qualities. In Egypt, tea is the national drink, and hibiscus leaves are a household staple.

Properties of plants for tea

You can grow plants selected for their taste or their medicinal properties. In most instances, the leaves of your herbs are harvested to make teas, however with some plants such as lemongrass, you can also use the flowers, roots and stems. These herbs are well known for their medicinal properties – and are also delicious.

Applemint (leaf) aids digestion and relaxes the stomach.

Calendula (flower) soothes inflamed skin, heals and cleanses.

Chamomile (flower) soothes and relaxes the gastrointestinal tract and nervous system.

Lemongrass (leaf) relaxes the stomach and intestinal muscles.

Liquorice (root) calms upset stomachs, cleanses the body and builds immunity.

Nettle (leaf) relieves arthritis, is a diuretic, and eases anemia and tiredness.

Peppermint (leaf) aids digestion, and soothes fevers and colds.

Rosemary (leaf) improves memory and concentration, relieves stress, improves liver function and helps to prevent cardiovascular disease.

Sage (leaf) eases menopausal flushing, improves memory and is good for sore throats and gum problems.

Yarrow (leaf) helps to heal wounds, treat coughs and colds, and aids an upset stomach.

Method

Rinse a handful of herbs in cold water, and strain. Put rinsed herbs into a teapot, cover with boiling water and infuse for 3–5 minutes. If you don't mind strong tea, you can leave the herbs in. Add honey, sugar and lemon to taste – and enjoy!

Drying leaves

Leaves can be harvested fresh from the plant, or dried. To prepare leaves for drying, wash them and shake off any excess moisture. Tie a handful of stems together and, with the leaves pointing downwards, hang in a cool dry spot in your home or garage. You'll know they have dried sufficiently when they crumble easily. Store them in a glass container or sealed plastic bag.

Make a tussie mussie

Herbs and flowers are more than just pretty faces; they harbour a secret language too. Since the 1400s, people have made and gifted tussie-mussies – small bouquets of herbs and flowers chosen for their meanings – to convey their sentiments in floral form.

GATHER HERBS / FLOWERS / LEAVES / SCISSORS / FLORAL TAPE / CARD / PEN

Say it with flowers

Tussie-mussies were popular in pre-revolutionary France, and on both sides of the Atlantic during the Victorian era. Every sprig and blossom in a tussie-mussie conveys a meaning in the language of flowers.

You can create beautiful, meaningful bouquets for yourself, or as gifts for friends and family. A wide variety of personal messages can be sent, from friendship, love and joy to mistrust, disappointment and even anger.

Popular flowers and their meanings

Here are some of the herbs and flowers that are popular in tussie-mussies, and their commonly accepted meanings.

Brambles – remorse

Blue violets – humility, modesty

Carnation – disappointment, rejection

Crocus – cheerfulness

Daisy – innocence, loyalty

Elderberry – sympathy

Goldenrod – encouragement

Grass – the fleeting quality of life

Ivy – fidelity

Lemon verbena – you have bewitched me

Lily of the Valley – return of happiness

Magnolia – nobility

Mint – don't worry about little things

Orchid – love, beauty, refinement

Palm leaves – victory and success

Pink rosebud – grace and beauty

Rosemary – remembrance

White chrysanthemum – truth

Making a tussie-mussie

Start by planning your message, then choosing and assembling the right herbs and flowers.

Trim all the stems to about 10 cm (4 in) long, then strip the leaves off the lower half of the stems.

Choose a prominent flower for the centre of your tussie-mussie, surround it with sprigs of herbs, then bind the stems together with some twine. Next, surround the central arrangement with alternate circles of herbs and flowers, securing each circle of stems with twine, until all your floral symbols have been included.

Once you're satisfied with your floral arrangement, trim all of the stems to the width of your palm, so the tussie-mussie can be comfortably held.

If you're making your tussie-mussie as a gift, write a little note or card to explain the concept and each of your floral or herbal choices.

Make scented mists and sprays

Flush with sweet smells, inviting aromas and heady scents, nature is the original perfumery, and people have been drawing on its abundance for inspiration and ingredients for centuries. Look to your own garden for pleasing scents to turn into mists and sprays for personal and household use.

GATHER FLOWER PETALS / CHEESECLOTH / BOWL / 1 CUP OF WATER / COOKING POT / STRAINER OR FUNNEL / SMALL GLASS SPRAY BOTTLE

As the name suggests, scented water is water with a floral aroma, made with flowers and herbs. Scented water is the original perfume, and has been used since Medieval times – although they were using it instead of soap for personal hygiene. Luckily, you can just use scented water as a rejuvenating mist or freshener. It can be misted or sprayed directly onto the skin, or even onto clothes and bed linen.

Which flowers to use?

To make your own perfumed water mists and sprays, gather fresh flower petals or buds. Mid-morning is the best time of day to do this, as the flowers will have warmed up and released their perfume, but won't be dried or wilted by the sun.

Gentle, cleansing rose and calming lavender are traditional favorites for scented water, but many different flowers can be steeped and turned into mists and sprays.

If you like refreshing citrus notes, gather lemon grass or lemon myrtle. Orange blossom offers citrus a sweet lift, while jasmine is rich and exotic.

You can also experiment with blending different flowers together to create your own signature sprays.

Method

1. Line your bowl with cheesecloth, allowing the edges to hang over by approximately 5 cm (2 in).

2. Place your gathered flower petals in the cheesecloth, then pour water on top – enough to make the cheesecloth sink to the bottom of the bowl and cover the flower petals.

3. Let them steep for at least 24 hours, then take the edges of the cheesecloth and draw them together. Your flower petals should all be contained in a little bundle in the cheesecloth. Gently pull the bundle out of the water and sit it in a clean bowl.

4. Pour the water from the bowl into a cooking pot, then take the cheesecloth bundle and gently squeeze any excess water into the pot.

5. Put the pot on the stove and turn on the heat. Bring the scented water to the boil then down to a simmer.

6. The longer you let your water simmer, the less scented water there will be … but the stronger the scent. If you plan to use your scented water as a room and household spray, simmer for a shorter amount of time to retain the volume. If you want it for personal use, let it simmer down until there are just a few teaspoons of liquid remaining.

7. Strain your scented water into an upcycled glass perfume or spray bottle and store it in the fridge to keep it cool and fresh.

Grow an avocado tree

Taking a seed and helping it to grow into a beautiful fruit-bearing plant is an easy way to help nature along. The seed (or pit) of an avocado is perfect for this – though be prepared to exercise your patience, as some pits never split open and sprout, so try growing a few at once.

GATHER AVOCADO PIT / TOOTHPICKS / A GLASS / WATER

Avocado pits can be germinated in soil, or in water. This water sprouting method is arguably the more common (and more charming) of the two, as you get to watch the sprout emerge, unfurl and flourish.

When a seed is germinated it splits open and a thirsty, sunshine- and nutrient-hungry sprout peeks out and begins to grow, and grow, and grow.

Propagate the pit

1. Remove the pit from inside a ripe, unrefrigerated avocado, rinse well and dry.

2. Push three or four toothpicks into the seed at its widest part, in a north, south, east, west pattern.

3. Suspend the pit over a glass of tepid water with the pointy end sticking up. The water should cover about an 2.5 cm (1 in) of the seed. The toothpicks will act as a miniature scaffold to support the pit's suspension; you might need to adjust them to make sure the pit is positioned correctly.

4. Put the glass in a warm place, like a sunny windowsill. The sun may soak up some of your water, so top up to maintain your water level. If you're lucky, the pit will stem in somewhere between two to six weeks. If it doesn't happen in this timeframe (which is quite common), try again with a new pit.

5. When the stem is about 15 cm (6 in) long, trim it in half.

Transplant the pit

1. When the stem sprouts back to its 15 cm (6 in) length, transplant the seedling to a pot with loose, sandy soil. Plant the seedling root down, leaving the top half of the pit sticking out of the soil.

2. Give your plant frequent, light watering and keep it in a sunny place to encourage growth.

3. Pinch back – use your fingers to break off – the newest top leaves every time the stems grow another 15 cm (6 in) or so to encourage more growth, and a fuller plant.

Note: some avocado plants can take years to bear fruit.

Grow heirloom tomatoes

Tomatoes that are grown from locally cultivated or saved seeds are called 'heirloom' or 'heritage'. They're often irregular in shape, size and color, and are sweet, flavorsome and succulent. So why not start your own family tradition, and give growing your own a go?

GATHER HEIRLOOM TOMATO SEEDLINGS / WOOD ASH (OPTIONAL) / WOODEN TOMATO STAKES FOR CLIMBING VARIETIES / HAMMER / MULCH / SOFT TWINE / WATERING CAN

The definition of what constitutes an 'heirloom' fruit or vegetable is a matter of debate. Some believe the seeds must be descended from plants that are more than 100 years old; others say from seed strains that pre-date the end of WWII, when hybrid seeds were widely introduced to commercial farming and home gardens.

Another way of defining heirloom fruit or vegetables is a cultivar that has been nurtured, selected, saved (see page 131) and handed down from one family or community member to another for many generations.

Heirlooms are open pollinated (pollinated naturally, without human intervention) and non-hybrid (not cross-pollinated; a common commercial practice). They are grown seasonally and today, because of the diligence of gardeners and growers like these, we can enjoy more than 20 varieties of heirloom tomatoes, many of which are not commonly or commercially available.

Get your own heirloom tomato crop started in spring once your soil has started to warm and there is no danger of frost.

Method

1. As the day draws to a close, find a warm and well-composted spot in your garden bed.

2. Make a hole the size of your fist, and place a handful of wood ash in it (optional, but desirable, as wood ash contains potassium, which improves fruit quality and helps to grow bigger, tastier tomatoes).

3. Gently tease apart your seedlings, keeping as much soil as possible on their roots. Plant them 1 m (39 in) apart, and firm down the soil around each.

4. Give your tomato seedlings a good soak, and gently place a light cover of mulch around each one.

5. For climbing tomatoes, hammer in a wooden stake to a depth of around 20 cm (8 in), roughly 10 cm (4 in) away from each tomato seedling. Bush varieties don't require staking. As your seedling grows, tie the stems to the stakes with soft twine. You can purchase twine from a nursery or hardware store, or make your own from old stockings.

6. Continue to tend your tomatoes lovingly, removing excess leaf growth to concentrate more energy into your tomatoes, and giving them a dose of liquid fertilizer once the flowers have set fruit.

7. Your tomatoes taste best when harvested ripe and warm on the vine, however you can also harvest them slightly under-ripe and let them come into their full sweetness in your kitchen.

8. To save seeds for planting next spring, slice a tomato, squeeze the pulp directly onto a paper towel and let dry. When you're ready to sow the seed, cut off a piece with four to six seeds on it and sow them in a pot.

Heirloom tomato and peach salad

This pretty salad's bright color is matched by an explosion of flavor, thanks to a tarty variety of heirloom tomatoes; the perfect match for the sweet peaches. Say hello to candy-like red cherry, fragrant orange beefsteak, dainty yellow pear, bold and juicy black Russian, and tangy and striking green zebra tomatoes.

SERVES 4

Salad

1 red onion, finely sliced

60 ml (¼ cup/2 fl oz) verjuice

400 g (1¾ cup/14 oz) mixed variety heirloom tomatoes, sliced

2 peaches, sliced into wedges

½ bunch of basil leaves, torn

Dressing

60 ml (¼ cup/2 fl oz) verjuice

1 tablespoon extra virgin olive oil

salt + pepper

Salad

1. Combine sliced red onion and 60 ml verjuice in a small bowl and set aside for 20 minutes to soften the flavor of the red onion. Drain, discarding the verjuice, and pat the red onion dry with paper towel.

2. Combine your mix of tomatoes, peaches, basil and soaked red onion in a bowl.

Dressing

1. Whisk together 60 ml verjuice with olive oil and salt and pepper to taste. Add to tomato mixture and toss gently to combine.

To serve

This salad could be served with some baked ricotta as an elegant appetizer, and try the leftovers as a bruschetta topping, on top of toasted bread spread with goats cheese. Best served fresh.

Create a terrarium

When Victorian-era botanist Nathaniel Bagshaw Ward accidentally sprouted a fern seed in a glass jar he was using for insect observation, he invented the terrarium. Growing tiny greens inside glass means you can watch plant growth in miniature, and it's a fun way to bring nature indoors.

GATHER PLASTIC VESSEL OR CONTAINER (GLASS WITH A LID IS PREFERABLE) / GRAVEL OR PEBBLES / SPHAGNUM MOSS / HORTICULTURAL CHARCOAL / COMMERCIAL (STERILIZED) POTTING MIX / TROPICAL AND SUB-TROPICAL PLANTS / STONES / DRIFTWOOD / DECORATIVE ITEMS (OPTIONAL)

Whether you want to green up your apartment or office space, creating your own garden ecosystem in a terrarium is an instantly rewarding solution.

The list of moisture-loving plants suited for terrariums is long (and lyrical) – pepperomia, syngonium, fittonia, callathea, spiderwort, parlour palms, club moss, selaginella, silver sprinkles and baby's tears …

Method

1. Clean your container with an anti-bacterial agent (dishwashing liquid is often enough) to ensure there are no harmful bacteria, fungi or algae present.

2. Start by adding a drainage layer of pebbles (most aquarium rocks will do the trick) to the bottom of the container. Make sure that you cannot see the bottom of your vessel through the drainage layer.

3. Firmly press moist sphagnum moss over your pebbles, ensuring that there are no gaps around the sides of the container. This layer will prevent the above living layers from contaminating the drainage, whilst also ensuring a source of moisture and a damp environment for your terrarium plant roots above.

4. Add a thin layer of horticultural charcoal, which will make sure your living layer (soil) doesn't sour over time.

5. Add your living layer of sterilized potting mix (most commercial potting mixes are already sterilized). You'll need to add at least 3–4 cm (1–2 in) of soil, but you can add a little more to your vessel for a hilly look. It's important that your soil is clean, otherwise fungi will quickly overrun your terrarium, due to its warm, damp environment.

6. Add your plants to your soil layer in whatever layout you like. Be creative – try and imagine the end result as you go. Group your taller plants towards the middle of your vessel. You can remove up to half of any plant's root ball (their root system, often shaped to the container they have grown up in) as they'll still get plenty of water in the moist environment of your terrarium.

7. Add stones, driftwood or other decorative items to your mini landscape as you see fit.

8. Mist/spray water on your plants and decorative items, as well as the sides of your container. This amount of water, in combination with the moisture from the sphagnum moss layer, will be enough to feed your plants. If your terrarium has a lid, keep the lid off until the plants are dry to the touch, then cover.

Tip: Ensure your terrarium layers take up no more than a third of your container, so that there is plenty of room for your plants to grow and thrive.

Terrarium maintenance

Once made, you should not need to add any water to your terrarium for many months. If your terrarium does not have a lid, you will need to water it regularly as you would any house plant.

Never over-water your terrarium. If you notice heavy condensation on the container lid or walls, remove the lid for up to a day at a time to allow the moisture to leave the vessel. If your plants are wilting, yellowing or look dry – mist them with your spray bottle.

Prune any overgrown plants, especially if they're growing up against the container walls as this can cause plants to rot and fester.

Ensure your terrarium is placed in a brightly lit spot, at least 50 cm (20 in) away from any direct sunlight. Rotate your terrarium occasionally to ensure your plants are getting an even dosage of sun.

Paint stones

Hold a smooth river stone in one palm and a paintbrush in the other, and see if you can resist putting the two together. Painted stones can be used as paperweights, plant decorations and children's toys, or simply framed as beautiful artworks.

GATHER STONES / ACRYLIC INK OR ACRYLIC PAINT / SMALL PAINTBRUSH / ACRYLIC MATT UV VARNISH/ LARGE WATERCOLOR BRUSH

To start, choose stones that are very smooth and beautifully rounded. Not only are they more pleasing to look at and to hold, but painting on a smooth stone is much easier than painting on a bumpy, uneven one. Wash the stones in warm, soapy water, rinse well and leave to dry naturally. When the stones are dry they'll be ready to paint on. Use acrylic paint or acrylic ink – this free-flowing ink makes it easier to paint fine details, and dries to a smooth, matt finish. You'll need a small brush with a fine point.

Draw inspiration from nature; you can paint anything from a tree to patterns found on a leaf. If you're new to this type of painting, start with simple patterns and work your way up to more complex designs as you become used to the feel of the brush and ink.

Once you have applied ink to stone, leave the ink to dry overnight.

The stones will then be ready for a coat of varnish to protect the design and to bring out the depth of color in the stone itself. Use a varnish that works on the sort of paint you have used, applying it with a larger, soft watercolor brush for an even coat. A matt varnish works best, as it doesn't interfere with the natural beauty of the stone.

When the varnish is dry, your stones will be ready to display either alone or as part of a collection.

Try experimenting with different combinations of stones, mixing various shapes, colors, or designs to create unique and striking collections.

Don't feel you have to stick to using just white paint either – you can paint a stone completely black first and then add the design on top in white for a more dramatic, graphic look, or play around with different colors. There are no rules, so just have fun.

gather

Blueberry and spelt galette with almond milk custard

Part of the beauty of a galette (a French tart consisting of a flat, round, flaky crust with a fruit topping) is its versatility - you can top the base with any summer berries or stone fruit. Its rustic charm also makes it a very forgiving pastry to make, and using spelt flour in place of regular flour adds a little extra earthiness in flavor.

SERVES 6

Spelt shortcrust

250 g (2¼ cups/9 oz) spelt flour

2 tablespoons raw caster sugar

½ teaspoon salt

125 ml (½ cup/4½ fl oz) sunflower oil

2 tablespoons iced water

Blueberry filling

300 g (1½ cups/11 oz) fresh or frozen blueberries

1 tablespoon arrowroot powder (or cornflour)

1 teaspoon lemon zest

2 teaspoons lemon juice

Almond milk custard

500 ml (2 cups/18 fl oz) almond milk

1 vanilla bean, split and seeds scraped

4 egg yolks

2 tablespoons arrowroot powder (or cornflour)

60 g (¼ cup/2 oz) raw sugar

Using oil in place of butter makes it easier and quicker to bring the pastry together in the humidity and heat of summer, when pastry making can be a sticky situation. The almond milk custard adds a creamy touch when serving, but is lighter in flavor and consistency than traditional custard.

Spelt shortcrust

1. Combine flour, sugar and salt in a large mixing bowl. Make a well in the centre and add the oil. Using a fork, mix the flour mixture into the oil until it is well combined and has the texture of small peas.

2. Sprinkle over the water and mix into the dough with your fingertips. It should be moist enough to just bring together – the drier the pastry the flakier the crust.

3. Using your fingers, bring the dough into a ball. Turn out onto a floured surface, flatten dough with a rolling pin and shape into a disk. Wrap in cling film, then transfer to a plate and refrigerate for at least 30 minutes.

Blueberry filling

1. While your pastry is chilling, combine blueberries, arrowroot, lemon zest and juice in a mixing bowl and toss thoroughly and gently with your fingers to combine.

Almond milk custard

1. Combine almond milk and vanilla seeds and bean in a saucepan over a medium-high heat. Bring just to the boil, then reduce and simmer for 1 minute. Remove from heat and set aside to infuse for 20 minutes.

2. In a separate saucepan, whisk egg yolks and arrowroot into a smooth paste. Add sugar and whisk until smooth and pale.

3. Strain almond milk mixture and return to a clean saucepan. Place over a medium-high heat and bring to scalding point. Pour the heated milk into the egg mixture and whisk to combine.

4. Place the saucepan of custard over a medium-low heat. Using a wooden spoon, slowly stir mixture until thick, about 3–5 minutes. Transfer to a bowl to serve warm or chilled. If serving chilled, wrap the bowl tightly with cling film to avoid a film forming on top of the custard.

To assemble the galette

1. Preheat oven to 200°C (400°F).

2. Remove pastry from cling film and sandwich between 2 sheets of baking paper. Roll until 3 mm (⅛ in) thick (about 34 cm [13 in] in diameter), then remove and discard the top layer of baking paper.

3. Gently pick up baking sheet topped with the pastry and transfer to a 32 cm (12½ in) wide baking tray. Top with the blueberry filling, leaving a 3 cm (1 in) gap around the edge. Gently fold over the pastry. It doesn't matter if it cracks a little, as the beauty of this tart is that it is characteristically 'rustic' looking.

4. Bake in preheated oven for 25–30 minutes, until pastry is golden.

5. Remove from oven and leave for 3 minutes to cool slightly, then transfer to a wire rack to cool. Give the blueberries a little shuffle on top to make sure they're all coated in the syrup.

6. Serve warm or cold with the almond milk custard on the side.

go on a picnic

waldeinsamkeit

A German term from the words *wald* (woods)
and *einsamkeit* (solitude), *waldeinsamkeit* is the feeling
of being alone in the woods, and at one with nature.

Meditate

More and more people are tuning into meditation as a way to counteract the busy-ness of modern life. Nature is busy too, but its comings and goings - the rising sun, the blowing wind, the sweeping tide - have their own steady and contemplative rhythm, and can be a wonderful focal point for mindfulness.

One of the aims of meditation is to learn how to be. It's not about trying or doing, but simply being, here and now. Go and be in nature ... your mind will thank you for it.

Be comfortable

Find a quiet place and arrange yourself in a way that feels right for you. This might mean sitting cross-legged with your back against a tree, or lying on the grass with the sun on your face. Allow your jaw to soften and your lips to part slightly.

Breathe

As you begin to settle, pay attention to the sounds you hear around you. After a few moments, shift your focus inwards and allow yourself to become absorbed by the in and out rhythm of your breath. Don't try to control it, just let it be.

Maintain a detached focus on the mind's meandering into the past and future, and on the body in place and time. Let your thoughts rise and fall like gentle waves. If they grow too big, return to the breath. Count five deep, slow breaths. Let it anchor your meditation. Where do you feel your breath? On your nostrils or your upper lip? In your chest or your belly?

Keep on breathing.

Have fun

Experiment and find your own meditation style. You can pick and choose from a range of meditation techniques championed by various mindfulness practitioners. Try:

• Sitting with a straight spine to encourage energy flow.

• Placing your tongue on the roof of your mouth, just behind the teeth, to relax the jaw.

• Sitting on a cushion, or not sitting on a cushion.

• Closing your eyes, or opening your eyes.

• Smiling gently, or not smiling gently.

• Encouraging your mind to feel grateful. What are you thankful for in this moment?

Start small

Don't sit down to meditate for an hour if it's going to be a strain. Start with a two or five or ten-minute meditation, then extend this out as your practice develops. Or not. It's up to you.

Set your intention - and your alarm. This will stop you from peeking at the clock to see how much time has passed. You'll eventually surrender to the ebb and flow of nature, and the time will tell itself.

FALL

smell the rain

The pleasant scent that imbues the air when rain is afoot is called 'petrichor'.
From the Greek 'petra' (stone) and 'ichor' (the ethereal blood of the gods),
it describes the smell of oils in rocks and soil being released by moisture from
the rain. Scientists have suggested that humans have inherited affection for
the smell from ancestors who relied on rainy weather for their survival.

Plant a native garden

Native and indigenous plants are perfectly suited to your soil and climate. They're easy to care for, kind on precious resources, and don't need much in the way of boosters. When you plant a native garden you're more likely to enjoy the company of native birds, animals and insects – just as nature intended.

GATHER YOUR CHOICE OF PLANTS FROM TUBESTOCK OR SMALL POTS / COMPOST / WEED TEAS / WORM JUICE / SLOW-RELEASE FERTILIZER

Indigenous plants are those found specifically in your local area, while native is a general term used to describe plants that are endemic or unique to your country.

This doesn't mean they can't be found in other countries, but once they've migrated, they're termed 'exotics'. For example, the voluptuous, heavily scented frangipani (*Hymenosporum flavum*) is native to Australia, but can be cultivated all over the world, from Europe and America to Asia and the Middle East.

Native and indigenous plants have spent hundreds, even thousands of years evolving in their local ecology: your particular soils, geology and climate. They've adapted to local conditions and naturally available nutrients, so why not invite them into your garden, and watch them thrive?

When to plant

Fall is the best time to plant your native and indigenous species because the weather is cooler and the fall and winter rain will help them to settle in.

Which plants to choose

Native plants come in all forms: groundcovers, climbers and herbs, grasses, smaller and larger shrubs, and trees. Some grow well in pots, while others like a lot of space. You might like to complement existing exotics, fruits and vegetables, or create an exclusively native garden.

Planting from tubestock or smaller pots is both cheaper and helps your plants get established faster.

Pick plants based on the space you have available, which species you are most attracted to, what habitat you wish to provide for insects, birds and animals and of course, where you live.

Care of native plants

Native and indigenous plants' inherent suitability to your existing conditions means that they don't need much in the way of additional nutrients – and that they might be sensitive to the extra nutrients in conventional fertilizers. Using well-matured compost, natural weed teas, worm juice and liquid, or small amounts of slow-release fertilizer can be enough to give your plants the boost they need until they are more fully established.

Don't think that because you're using native plants you need to replicate natural bushland or forest. Native plants can be manipulated, clipped and trained, just like their exotic cousins.

Where to start

To find out more about what plants are suited to your location and how to care for them, get in touch with your local authority or nursery. They often have guides to basic identification, cultivation, plant sizes and general care of natives.

Watch birds

Despite their delicate plumage, birds are some of nature's hardiest creatures.
They're descended from dinosaurs, and they've diversified into around 10,000
species. Bird watchers are called birders, and sometimes twitchers -
that's someone who will travel a long way to observe a rare bird
and tick it off their list of 'must see' birds.

Attract birds

Attracting birds to your garden or outdoor space is a wonderful way to show our feathered friends some love – from a respectful distance. These simple bird-feeding baubles are fun to make, they keep well, and are a safe and gentle way to invite birds into your world.

GATHER TABLESPOON / GELATINE / WATER / LARGE COOKING POT / BIRDSEED / BROWN OR WAX PAPER / COOKIE CUTTERS, MASON JAR LIDS OR MOULDS / SCISSORS / DRINKING STRAWS / STRING

How to make a bird-feeding bauble

This method makes six shapes measuring approximately 7.5 cm^2 (3 in^2). To make more or less, adjust the ingredients up or down. Note: this is a two-day project.

1. Start by sprinkling four tablespoons of gelatine over ½ cup of cold water. Let it sit for a few minutes, until the water has absorbed the gelatine.

2. While you wait, heat 1¾ cups of water in a pot, then stir the gelatine mixture in until it is dissolved.

3. Stir in 3 cups of birdseed (see recipe), and let the mixture stand and cool until the gelatine thickens and coats all the birdseed. This should take about 15 minutes.

4. Place your brown paper or wax paper on a flat surface, and arrange your cookie cutters, moulds or mason jar lids on it.

5. Once the mixture has thickened sufficiently and is cool enough for you to touch, pack the birdseed mixture inside your arranged shapes. Start by spooning the birdseed in, then use your fingers to press it into place. It should be firmly and evenly packed.

6. Cut your straw into pieces approximately 5 cm (2 in) long, then push a piece of straw through each shape – about 2 cm (⅘ in) from the edge and right through the birdseed – to the paper underneath. This will form the hole you'll thread your string through for hanging the bird feeder.

7. Leave the shapes to harden overnight in a cool, dark place. The next day, gently remove the straws and push the hardened birdseed shapes out of their moulds. Thread a piece of string through each hole, then hang them outside. Be mindful of how and where birds feed – make sure the baubles are accessible, and out of reach of predators. Now, wait … and enjoy watching the birds come calling.

Birdseed recipe

You can use commercial birdseed for this project – but why not make your own? It's easy: just gather 1 cup each of sunflower seeds (with the hulls still on), cracked corn, unsalted peanuts, and raisins or other dried fruit, like apples. Chop or blend each of the ingredients up so they're small like sunflower seeds, then mix them together.

photograph nature

———

"Photography is a medium, a language, through which I
might come to experience directly, live more closely with,
the interaction between myself and nature."

— PAUL CAPONIGRO

Save seeds

As long as there has been farming, there has been seed saving. People have been carefully gathering, saving and exchanging seeds from plants and trees for around 12,000 years, and you can continue in this tradition by saving seeds from your garden to sow in years to come.

GATHER LETTUCE PLANTS / BOWL / PAPER ENVELOPES OR SACHETS / PEN

The practice of seed saving is ancient, and simple … and even more important these days to maintain the diversity of the planet. It's an essential part of keeping the world and its innumerable populations healthy. Plus it's beautiful to be involved in the stewardship of a plant from seed to seed, nurturing and enjoying it through its life, and being an active part of its ongoing propagation.

You'll also be maintaining your most loved edible plants and flowers. Over time, these seeds will adapt to your particular place, climate and soil. The plants you grow from these seeds will have a better chance of thriving, provided you can keep enough genetic diversity in the seeds you save.

Some seed varieties only have limited availability, and are therefore very precious – seeds passed down by relatives or those from a special plant in a friend's garden. Seeds like these are called heirlooms: an old variety that has been maintained and nurtured by generations of seed saving.

Getting started

First, you need to grow the plant you'd like to save seeds from. If you're purchasing the seeds for this plant, make sure they're heirloom or open-pollinated (pollinated naturally, without human intervention) seeds, and not hybrids. Hybrid seeds have cross-pollinated with other seed varieties (such as broccoli and cauliflower), and you cannot guarantee what the next generation of plants will be like. It's also desirable to preserve heirloom varieties to support a greater range of vegetables, herbs and flowers than is commonly available.

Some plants, like corn, require more effort and a large number of plants to effectively save seeds. Begin with simpler, self-pollinating plants like lettuce, peas or cilantro, and only grow one variety at a time.

Saving lettuce seeds

1. When your lettuce plant is ready to go to seed, it will bolt. The leaves will lengthen and go bitter, and the plant will send up a tall stalk. Small yellow flowers will give way to dandelion-like fluff growing out of the seeds. Once the seeds look dry and darken in color they are ready to collect, usually in 2–4 weeks.

2. Gently cut off the flowering stalk and with the head down, dislodge the seeds into a bowl. You'll notice there are plant stems and chaff along with your seeds.

3. Now you get to winnow your seeds. Winnowing is an ancient technique for separating grains or seeds from chaff. The seeds will be heavier than the chaff in your bowl, so gently blow over the seeds to remove as much chaff as possible.

4. Put your cleaned seeds into a fresh, dry envelope and write down the variety of lettuce, the date, and spot in the garden where your seeds were saved from.

5. Store your seeds in a cool, dry, dark place, and make sure you use them within 2–3 years.

Go scrumping

Scrumpers know something scrumptious when they see it. Make the most of nature's bounty by following the lead of the scrumpers – modern day mavericks who scout out, map, harvest and eat the fruits, herbs and vegetables growing in public spaces that would otherwise go to waste.

Once upon a time, when people grew or traded all their own food, scrumping was an illicit activity akin to stealing. Today, it's the pastime of a new generation of eco-conscious urban dwellers who have playfully adopted this old English term for taking fruit from orchards, and applied it to the practice of harvesting fruit growing in public places, or collecting fruit that has already fallen on the ground.

What to scrump

There are two types of fruit that are up for scrumping: fruit growing in private gardens hanging over the fence into a public space, and feral fruit – that's fruit growing on roadsides, in culverts, along river and creek lines, next to bridges, and so on.

Of course, anything edible that's growing in a public space is up for scrumping, so you might get lucky and find nuts, herbs and vegetables to scrump, too.

Where to scrump

In the city, old or well established inner suburbs are hot spots for foraging overhanging fruit trees on streets and laneways. Undeveloped urban fringes can also be good for scrumping, especially if they were once used for farming.

In the country, apples, pears, walnuts often pop up on roadside strips, thanks to the wind carrying seeds, or people discarding fruit while driving.

Seasoned scrumpers advise against harvesting in industrial areas, as the fruit might be growing in contaminated soil, or have been exposed to airborne toxins.

When and how to scrump

Generally speaking, fruit trees are ready for harvest from midsummer through to late fall.

There's no need to be secretive about your scrumping, but do be mindful of social etiquette. If the fruit from a tree in a private garden has dropped to the footpath, the social (and legal) rules of scrumping state that you don't need to ask. But if the fruit is still hanging on the tree, and you want to pick more than one or two pieces, it's always polite to knock at the door and explain what you're up to. You might even offer to take back a sample of the jam or pie you make with your bounty.

Make a scrumping map

Find, print or sketch a map of your neighborhood and mark the location of scrumping spots to share with like-minded friends – or as a handy resource for yourself, come next scrumping season.

Get creative and design a key for your map that makes it clear what is available where. You might color code your markings to show what type of fruit is growing there, or draw a miniature apple, for an apple tree, a fig for a fig tree, and so on.

Happy scrumping!

Preserve abundance

Waste not, want not: preserving summer berries, tomatoes and stone fruits ensures you'll have a well-stocked pantry all year round. Turn the season's sweet, juicy bounty into jams, pickles and chutneys, or try your hand at some other preserving methods.

GATHER GLASS JARS WITH LIDS / BERRIES OR STONE FRUITS / LEMON JUICE / GRANULATED SUGAR / LARGE COOKING POT / STIRRING SPOON / NON-IODIZED SALT / WHITE DISTILLED OR CIDER VINEGAR WITH 5% ACIDITY / CUCUMBERS / PEPPERCORNS / FRESH DILL

Before modern living gave us electricity, refrigeration, large-scale farming, supermarkets and our favorite foods available all year round, people grew their own fruits, vegetables and herbs. They lived simply and seasonally, and preserved foods during times of abundance to help provide sustenance over winter, until spring and summer returned with new life and growth.

At a basic level, preservation prevents the growth of bacteria, fungi and other microorganisms by slowing or stopping the oxidation of fats that cause rancidity.

Methods vary by geographical location, culture, technology, ingredient and food preferences. Some are ancient methods that involve little resource use (but lots of elbow grease), while others rely on modern technology and devices. Common types include drying, cooling, freezing, heating, salting, sugaring, smoking, pickling, canning, bottling, jellying, jugging, burial, curing, and fermenting.

Jams, preserves and chutneys

These three variations on the theme of preserving in jars all involve boiling produce with sugar and sealing it in jars, but are different enough to warrant their own names.

Jams and preserves are both sweet. Jams use mashed up fruit, while preserves use whole or large pieces of fruit. Chutneys follow a similar method, but the core ingredients of tomatoes, apples, onions, herbs and spices and the like make chutneys a condiment more suited to the savory end of the food spectrum.

Basic method for jams, preserves and chutneys

Quantities and methods vary between recipes, but the basic cooking method is the same.

Prepare your jars and lids by washing them in soapy water, then rinsing them in clean water and placing the jars (not the lids) in an oven tray, and baking them at 110°C (230°F) to sterilize them. The lids should simply be placed in a bowl of hot, clean water until they are needed (hot jams and preserves should be bottled in hot jars; cooled ones in cold jars).

Wash the fruit or vegetable, removing any stems, cores, pits and blemishes. Peel it, if necessary – cherries and berries do not require peeling (but cherry pits should be removed); whereas apples, peaches and pears do. To make a jam, cut up or mash the fruit. For a preserve, use the fruit whole or cut it into large chunks. You can use vegetables or fruit for a chutney; cut these into chunks.

Place all the fruit or vegetable in a large pot, measuring it in cup by cup. Then, for every cup of fruit or vegetable, add ¾ cup of sugar. If you are using ripe or particularly sweet fruit, add 1–2 tablespoons of lemon juice, as the acid from the lemon juice will help it to thicken. When making chutney, you'll also need to add vinegar. The amount of vinegar you should add depends on the fruit or vegetable – and also the type of vinegar. You can use cider vinegar, balsamic, red wine … Try making chutney using the millilitre equivalent to your grams of sugar and adjust to taste.

Place the pot on the stove. Bring the mixture to a boil then turn it down to a simmer.

Stir it often, making sure that it doesn't burn or stick to the pot. The mixture will need to simmer for 30–120 minutes; until it holds its shape when you take a small amount out of the pot on a teaspoon. Once this has happened, carefully pour it into the sterile jars and seal the lids. Then label and date your jars and store them in a cool, dark, dry place. They will keep for months, even years, but once opened should be stored in the fridge and consumed within the month.

Pickles

Pickling is another tried and tested means of food preservation. It works by either immersing food in vinegar or fermenting it in brine to lower its pH (acid) level to 4.6 or below, thus preserving it. All fruits except figs, most tomato varieties and a host of vegetables are suited to pickling – try this method with fresh cucumber.

Basic method for pickling cucumbers

Begin by scrubbing the cucumbers well. Dry them, then remove and discard a 0.6 cm (¼ inch) slice from the blossom end (as the blossoms can contain an enzyme that causes the pickles to become too soft). Slice them evenly, and layer in a clean, sterile jar – use the same method to sterilize jars as for jams and preserves. As you layer the slices of cucumber, place fresh dill leaves and whole peppercorns between each layer. Do not fill the jar right to the top, but leave a space of about 1.5 cm (½ inch) at the top.

Next, combine water, vinegar and salt in a saucepan – enough to fill the jar or jars you are using, in the following proportions: 3 cups water to ½ cup vinegar to 1½ tablespoons salt.

Bring the mixture to the boil over a medium-high heat then carefully pour it over the cucumbers in the jar. Seal the jar immediately, then label and date your jars and store them in a cool, dark, dry place.

Let the pickles mellow for at least three weeks before opening; once the jar has been opened, store it in the refrigerator, where it will last several months.

This basic method can be applied to a range of other vegetables. Experiment with different herbs and spices: try green beans with cayenne pepper, garlic and dill, cauliflower with cumin, turmeric, garlic and bay leaf, or eggplant with oregano, thyme, black pepper and chilli flakes – or create your own flavorsome batch.

Pickling tips

The best salt to use is one intended for canning or pickling salt or at a pinch, non-iodized salt. This is because iodized salt makes the brine cloudy. It can also change the color and texture of the vegetables, and may leave sediment at the bottom of the jars.

The best vinegar to use is a white distilled or cider vinegar with 5% acidity. This helps to bring the pH of the pickles to the right level. When pickling lighter colored vegetables, like cauliflower, use a white vinegar to retain (or remain close to) the original color.

For crisper pickles, put the vegetables (whole or sliced) into a wide bowl and spread a layer of pickling salt on top. Cover with a clean tea towel and let sit overnight in a cool place. Discard any liquid, then rinse and dry the vegetables before pickling or canning as usual. The salt helps to pull the moisture out of the vegetables and makes them crisper.

Buckwheat crepes with pears and figs

This is a rich and earthy brunch dish, featuring the brown, purple and fawn colors of fall. Rather than sugar and butter, this caramel is made sweet with dates, and creamy and rich by the coconut milk, oil and tahini. Thyme brings a lemony and minty savouriness, adding some edge to the sweetness of the dish.

SERVES 4

Date and tahini caramel
MAKES ABOUT 2 CUPS
155 g (1 cup/5½ oz) dates
1 tablespoon tahini
80 ml (⅓ cup/3 fl oz) coconut milk
2 tablespoons coconut oil, melted
1 teaspoon vanilla
1 tablespoon maple syrup
⅛ teaspoon salt, or more to taste

Buckwheat crepes
MAKES ABOUT 12 CREPES
300 g (2¼ cups/11 oz) buckwheat flour
2 eggs
250 ml (1 cup/9 fl oz) milk
250 ml (1 cup/9 fl oz) water
butter or oil, for frying
figs, to serve

Honey and thyme roasted pears
4 beurre bosc pears, halved and cored
3 tablespoons honey
3 tablespoons water
1 teaspoon thyme leaves
cinnamon
20 g (⅘ oz) butter

Date and tahini caramel

1. Cover the dates with 250 ml (1 cup/ 8 fl oz) boiling water and leave to sit and soften for 10 minutes. Drain, reserving liquid.

2. Combine the drained dates, tahini, coconut milk, coconut oil, vanilla, maple syrup and salt in a blender or food processor and blend until smooth. Add enough of the reserved water to make a creamy and smooth caramel.

Buckwheat crepes

1. Combine flour, eggs and milk together in a mixing bowl or blender. Whisk or beat with electric beaters until smooth. Cover with cling film and set aside to rest for at least an hour, or overnight. Resting the batter will allow the air bubbles created in the batter when whisking to dissipate, making the crepes stronger and less likely to tear when cooking.

2. Cook your crepes when your pears are just out of the oven (see overleaf). Heat a 23 cm (9 in) wide frying pan or crepe pan over a medium-low heat – you don't want the pan too hot as it will cause the batter to cook too quickly which can create holes. Coat the pan with a little oil and heat. Add ¼ cup of batter and cook for a couple of minutes on one side, then flip and cook on the other side. Each side should look golden brown when done.

3. Transfer to a plate to serve, then repeat with remaining batter.

Honey and thyme roasted pears

1. Heat oven to 190°C (375°F). Place pears, skin side down, on a baking tray. Add water to tray, drizzle honey over the pears, sprinkle with thyme leaves and cinnamon and dot with butter. Cover with foil and roast for 30 minutes. Remove foil and roast for a further 10–15 minutes, until golden.

2. Remove pears from liquid, reserving honey liquid to serve.

To serve

1. In a large saucepan over a medium-low heat, add caramel, 1 tablespoon brandy and 125 ml (½ cup/4 fl oz) boiling water to loosen the mixture. Whisk to combine. Sprinkle thyme leaves over mixture, then lay the pear slices in the pan and sprinkle cinnamon over the pears. Reduce heat to low and allow to cook for about 7–10 minutes, until caramel is bubbling and pears are soft.

2. Divide crepes and pears between 4 plates. Serve with wedges of fresh fig and a little warmed coconut milk.

Forage for edible weeds

Weeds are perhaps the most misunderstood members of nature's pantry. Called 'common' for their abundance and often pulled out of the ground (literally, weeded!) for their resilience, their potential as a source of fresh, tasty and readily available nourishment is worth exploring and foraging for.

GATHER EDIBLE WEED GUIDE / BASKET OR BAG / SECATEURS / LONG SLEEVES / GLOVES

Many plants commonly considered weeds – mainly because they spring up without being planted or cultivated, and spread with ease – are in fact edible. And not only are they edible, they're full of nutrition and unique flavor.

Edible weeds can be enjoyed in salads, soups, stir-fries, desserts and teas. Like their cultivated cousins, the younger leaves of wild leafy greens are tenderer and often less bitter than older leaves.

Foraging knowledge

Edible weeds may be growing in your garden, or in a nearby park or nature corridor. Like any other edible plant (or herb or fruit) they can be foraged, prepared and eaten. However, if you're foraging outside your own garden, it's important to be certain that any weeds you gather have not been sprayed with herbicides, or grown in polluted soil or water.

It's also important to be certain that you are identifying plants correctly, and note that only some parts of some weeds are edible. If you're not already an expert on plants, perhaps you know someone who is, who would love to share their knowledge of plants and foraging with you. For example, they might recommend long sleeves and a pair of gloves for harvesting blackberries, prickly pear or nettle, as they can prickle or sting.

Otherwise, consult a book on the topic – preferably one written about your geographical location.

Popular edible weeds

Here are some of the more readily available and popular edible weeds, along with details of which parts are edible, their nutritional properties and medicinal properties (if any).

Dandelion is high in minerals, vitamins and cancer-fighting antioxidants. All parts are edible, from the yellow petals (great in salads) to the root. Its fresh young leaves are lovely cooked, or make an excellent addition to salads. Its roots can also be dried and brewed into a tasty hot beverage.

Nettles are particularly high in calcium. The leaves can be used as a blood tonic, the sting to treat arthritis, and the roots for treating an enlarged prostate. Remove the sting by wilting the leaves and stems in boiling water for 30 seconds. You can make soup from the leaves and stems, or use the leaves as a substitute for cooked spinach in a favorite recipe, or dry the leaves for tea.

Watercress is high in vitamins K, C and A. It helps to form and strengthen bones, is helpful in treating Alzheimer's, improves iron deficiency, and aids the body in fighting infections. All of this delicate plant can be eaten; use it as a salad green, steam it, have it in a sandwich, or put it in soups to add a subtle peppery flavor.

Other commonly available and rather tasty 'weeds' to learn about are blackberries, chickweed, fennel, mallow, nasturtium and prickly pear.

Beet gnocchi with nettle pesto

Pesto is a great way to use up the masses of leafy greens and herbs that grow like triffids in fall. You can use different combinations of the greens and herbs with various oils, nuts, seeds, lemon juice or vinegar for some acidity, and garlic and cheese for depth.

SERVES 4-6

Nettle pesto
MAKES ABOUT 2½ CUPS

1 large bunch stinging nettle leaves, to yield about 75 g (4 cups/2½ oz) leaves

60 g (⅔ cup/2 oz) almonds, roasted*

150 ml (⅗ cup/5 fl oz) olive oil

60 g (⅔ cup/2 oz) parmesan cheese, grated

½ garlic clove, crushed

1 teaspoon lemon juice, to taste

salt + pepper

Beet gnocchi

150 g (5 oz) beets, boiled until soft

500 g (18 oz) potatoes

1 egg

200 g (1⅔ cups/7 oz) plain flour

2 tablespoons oil

This pesto version uses nettle, which grows in abundance along riverbeds and in backyards towards the end of fall, when the temperatures drop and rain has been falling (see previous page). Although it's usually picked out and discarded as a weed, blanching nettles in boiling water will remove the sting, and it can be used in cooking in the same way as spinach. The taste is somewhere between spinach, broccoli and cucumber, and it's rich in iron and calcium. As a substitute in this dish, rocket and mizuna would work well as they bring a little pepperiness to the sweetness of the beet gnocchi.

Nettle pesto

1. Using gloves, pick off the leaves from the nettle stems, discarding stems. Bring a large saucepan of water to the boil, add leaves for about 30 seconds, then drain and refresh under cold water.

2. Squeeze the leaves dry and then roughly chop. Combine chopped nettle leaves, almonds, olive oil, garlic and parmesan in a food processor and blend until smooth. Add lemon juice, salt and pepper to taste.

*Almonds can be roasted in a saucepan over a medium heat and cooked on each side for about 2-3 minutes. They can also be toasted in an oven, at 190°C (375°F) spread out on a tray lined with baking paper, for about 5-8 minutes, stirring occasionally to ensure even cooking.

Beet gnocchi

1. Preheat oven to 200°C (400°F). Roast potatoes in their skins for about 1 hour, until soft enough that a fork can be easily inserted. Allow to cool just enough to be able to handle, then peel and transfer to a large mixing bowl.

2. Pass the potatoes through a ricer or mash with a potato masher until smooth.

3. Cover beets with water in a small saucepan. Boil until soft enough that a skewer inserted goes through easily. Once cool enough to handle, top and tail and peel the beets, then chop roughly.

4. In a food processor or blender, blend beets to a fine puree.

5. Add beet puree and whisked egg to the potato and mix together with a wooden spoon until thoroughly combined. Add flour and bring the mixture together into a ball.

6. Turn the mixture onto a floured surface and knead gently for 1–2 minutes, until the dough is smooth and evenly colored.

7. Divide dough into six portions. Roll each portion out into logs about 2 cm (⅘ in) wide. If you're using a gnocchi board** to shape the gnocchi, cut into pieces about 1.5 cm (½ in) wide, then roll along board to shape. If you're using a fork to shape the gnocchi, cut the pieces a little thicker, about 2 cm (⅘ in), then press with a fork to indent. Scoring the gnocchi is not essential but allows them to hold sauce better.

8. Prepare a large tray dusted with flour or lightly oiled. Heat a large saucepan of water. Add gnocchi in batches, without overcrowding the pan. The gnocchi are cooked once they rise to the surface, after about 2 minutes. Remove with a slotted spoon and transfer to prepared tray. Repeat with remaining gnocchi and reserve the cooking water.

9. Heat oil in a large saucepan over a medium-high heat. Add gnocchi and fry for about 2 minutes, stirring or shaking the pan so that the gnocchi crisps up on all sides. Add pesto and a few tablespoons of the cooking water and cook until pesto has warmed through, turning gently when needed.

10. Divide between plates to serve.

**These are available from kitchen stores and online.

ride a bike

—

'It is by riding a bicycle that you learn the contours of a country best,
since you have to sweat up the hills and coast down them.'

— ERNEST HEMINGWAY, *BY-LINE, ERNEST HEMINGWAY*

Make a kite

When kites were invented in China around 2000 years ago, they were originally made from silk and bamboo – but it wasn't long before aerodynamic marvels made of paper were seen dancing in the skies too. Harness the power of the wind with this classic diamond-shaped paper kite. Up, up and away!

GATHER DOWEL / HANDSAW / RULER / PENCIL / FILE / BALL OF STRING / ONE PIECE OF TISSUE PAPER 100 x 100 CM (39 x 39 IN) / SCISSORS / WASHI TAPE / PLIERS / CRAFT KNIFE / CRAFT MAT / SCRAP FABRIC

Making the frame

Use your handsaw to cut two lengths of dowel; one 50 cm (20 in) long (the spar) and the other 56 cm (22 in) long (the spine). Next, take your ruler and pencil and mark the halfway point along the spar (25 cm [10 in]), and the quarter point along the spine (14 cm [5½ in]). Lay the spar to sit horizontally across the spine, intersecting the two marked points. Tie the spar and spine together by winding some string around in an X formation. Tie a double knot and trim the excess.

Carefully cut a notch about 3 mm (⅛ in) deep across each end of the spar and spine (that's four notches in total). This is so you can secure your string around the outside.

Cut 180 cm (71 in) of string and slide it through each notch, creating a diamond shape around the edge of the kite, until you reach the beginning of the length of string. Make sure that the string is taut on all four sides, then tie the ends together, secure them with a double knot, and trim the excess.

Making the sail

Put a sheet of tissue paper down flat. Place the frame on top of the tissue paper and trace lightly around it with your pencil, then lift the frame away. Next, draw a diamond shape 2 cm (⅘ in) bigger than your first diamond shape. Use scissors to cut this bigger diamond out, then put the frame back in place.

Working on one side of the frame at a time, fold the 2 cm (⅘ in) tissue paper border over the string and tape it down, at each corner of your kite.

Making the keel

Cut two 1 m (39 in) long pieces of string. Tie one 15 cm (6 in) from the bottom of the spine, and another above where the spine and spar meet. Secure each one with a double knot.

Hold the top string vertically away from the kite, then bring the second string up in the air to meet it – double knot the ends of the two pieces of string together.

Making the tail

Tape strips of scrap tissue paper or long pieces of washi tape (folded back on itself to prevent it from sticking) to the bottom of the spine; this is the tail.

Making the flying line

Cut 5–10 m (197–394 in) of string, depending on how high you want your kite to soar. Tie one end of the string to the keel with a double knot, and wrap the other end around a stick.

Dig for clay

Humans have been finding and digging for clay to shape into vessels, pottery and craft pieces on the edges of lakes, rivers, creeks and streams for thousands, even millions, of years. It's a simple and extremely satisfying practice, and a wonderful excuse to get some dirt between your toes.

GATHER PENKNIFE / BUCKET / SHOVEL OR TROWEL / HAMMER / WATER / SIEVE / BOARD OR TABLE TOP / PLASTIC ZIP-LOCK BAG

Clay is a fine-grained, highly malleable natural rock or soil material that becomes hard when dried or fired. Its color can range from white to dull grey, to brown or a deep orange-red, depending on its mineral content.

Where to find clay

Clay can be found wet, or dry. It is often found around lakes, creeks, rivers or streams – particularly in the lower parts or edges, where the water is calm and still, or in dry river and creek beds. It can also be found where road construction crews and builders have cleared away the topsoil.

When you go looking for clay, ask permission if you want to enter private land. Be careful around waterways, and never dig for clay in environmentally polluted or unstable areas.

How to recognize and dig for clay

In its dry state, clay may look like dirt or rocks; in its wet state, like mud. If you find dry lumps that you think might be clay, take a chunk and scrape it with your penknife. If it's clay, the fine particles will crumble off. Scrape some into a small pile and dampen with water to see if it dissolves – if it does, you've found clay.

In a wet area, clear and dig beneath layers of leaves, sand, stones and humus. You'll know you're at or near clay when the mud or soil becomes fine and grainy. Test it by taking a small lump and working it into a ball with your fingers. Roll it into a 'worm', then coil it around your finger. If it stays

together and feels smooth and plastic, you've found clay. Use your trowel or shovel to gather what you need into your bucket. Take care not to add stones, twigs or dirt.

How to prepare the clay for use

If the clay is clean, and with good plasticity, you'll be able to use it. But often, found clay needs to be processed.

Begin by spreading out your haul and letting it dry – note that this could take up to a week. When it has dried completely, use a hammer to break it up into pea-sized pieces. Then, fill a bucket with as much water as you have clay. Sprinkle the clay into the water and stir. Add more water to make a liquid mass, then let it sit for at least a few hours.

Stir the mixture well then sieve it into another bucket through a sieve or flyscreen, adding water to keep the mixture moving through the sieve. Leave the sieved clay to settle in the bucket, then pour off any extra water. Repeat until the clay is mud-like. Use a trowel to spread it out on a board (an old formica table top is perfect). When it's stiff enough to roll, knead and fold until it feels pliable (this is called 'wedging'). Now it's time to store it.

Storing your clay

Separate the wedged clay into workable chunks. Wrap each chunk tightly in several layers of plastic, and put it in an airtight zip-lock bag or similar and tightly closed bag. It can be kept this way for months, even years.

Pinch pots

Nature is rarely symmetrical, ordered or tidy – and neither are these handmade clay pinch pots. They're deliberately textured and uneven, and are just the thing for planting succulents, housing stone collections and whatever else you need a little nature-inspired treasure trove for.

GATHER CLAY / WATER / DECORATING TOOLS / ACRYLIC PAINT /
PAINTBRUSHES / VARNISH (OPTIONAL)

All clay is different. Just some of the variables that have formed your clay are where it comes from; what types of rocks, soils, minerals and oxides have come together over thousands, even millions of years to form it; and how it has been collected, prepared and stored. To find clay see previous page.

Shaping your pinch pot

Begin by kneading and warming your clay. Get to know it. Is it dry and crumbly, or wet and pliable? You want it to be wet (but not too wet), so if it's dry, add a little water. If it's too wet, add some soil.

When the clay is warm, and free of air pockets and has good plasticity (the potter's term for clay that is flexible and good to work with), roll it into a ball.

Push your thumb down into the centre of the ball of clay and create a hole. Work through the hole until it is around 1 cm (²⁄₅ in) from the bottom of the ball of clay, then use your thumb and index finger to pinch and press the clay outwards and upwards. With each movement of your fingers, your pot should begin to take shape. Turn it as you pinch to maintain a (relatively) even thickness in the walls, and in the overall shape of the pot.

Take your time to work the pot into a shape that appeals to you, then flatten the bottom by carefully pressing it against a table or a flat work surface. You might want to create small feet for your pot, or leave it flat.

Pay attention to the lip of the pot; it doesn't have to be perfect, but don't let it get too thin, as this is the part that will probably weather the most wear and tear.

Decorating and finishing

Use your fingers to smooth out the surface of the pot, then get creative. Household items like spoons, knives and toothpicks, and foraged items like shells, sticks and twigs all make good decorating tools. Potters use all sorts of tools to achieve finished effects on their creations – brass hole cutters, bevel cutters, ribs, pin tools, knives. One of the lovely things about working with clay is that you can rework it, so don't be afraid to experiment. Try pressing the end of a pencil into the clay to create pockmarks, running a pointy twig through the clay to create patterns, or pressing a leaf into the clay to make an imprint.

When you're happy with your pinch pot, place it somewhere warm on a windowsill for a few days, and let it dry. Fire it, if you can – take it to your local ceramic workshop – otherwise finish it in a way that appeals to you: by using a fine sandpaper to smooth the surface and edges, by decorating it with acrylic paint, and, if you want a glossy finish, a coat of varnish too.

Safety note: take care not to put food in vessels that have not been glazed with a food-safe glaze.

Print leaves

Fall is the season when deciduous trees shed their leaves
(a process called abscission) in strategic, survivalist anticipation of the winter
ahead. Collecting these fallen glories to use in printmaking means you can
synchronize your creative self with the seasons.

GATHER FALL LEAVES / OLD NEWSPAPER / INK OR PAINT / PAPER, CARD OR FABRIC / PAINTBRUSHES
OR INK SPONGES / INK BRAYER (ROLLER) / CLEAN CLOTH / SMALL JAR OF WATER

Leaf prints can be used for many decorative purposes, from creating art on archival paper and framing it, to customising fabric for crafting onto bags, teatowels and t-shirts.

Finding the right leaves

Leaves come in all shapes, sizes and textures, so look for variety as you ramble and forage. Leaves can be plucked from plants and trees to use in this project at any time of year. If the tree is an evergreen, you'll need to pick them directly from the tree, even in fall.

If you are foraging for fallen autumn leaves, look for newly fallen leaves. Fresh, pliable leaves are best for this project, as dried leaves will snap and crumble when pressed or worked on.

Preparing for printing

Start by laying newspapers down to protect your work surface. Then lay out your materials: your paints or inks, your paintbrushes or ink sponges and ink brayer, and the paper or card you plan to print on to. A clean cloth and a jar of water for wiping up any spills might also come in handy.

Next, prepare your masters – that's printmaking speak for the object that will create the impression you're printing out: your leaves. They need to be dry for your printmaking session.

Printing leaves

Select a leaf, then take a good look at it. Is it bumpy or smooth? Are there any ridges? Is one side different from the other? The markings will form the print pattern.

Take a paintbrush or ink sponge and apply some paint to the leaf. Once the leaf is fully and evenly covered, gently turn it over and press it onto the paper. You can press it down with your hands, or roll an ink brayer along its surface. When you're done, lift the leaf away slowly and admire your work.

Being playful

You don't need to be too prescriptive with your prints, as each leaf is able to make about six prints. Wipe the leaf clean with a cloth between applications, for best effect.

Some things to try:

- Apply a lot of paint, and then a little.
- Print each side of the leaf.
- Push down hard when you roll or press the leaf, then push down very, very softly.
- Hold the leaf flat to prevent movement, then let it go.
- Roll or press in all directions, then in just one direction.
- Overlay leaf prints on top of each other.

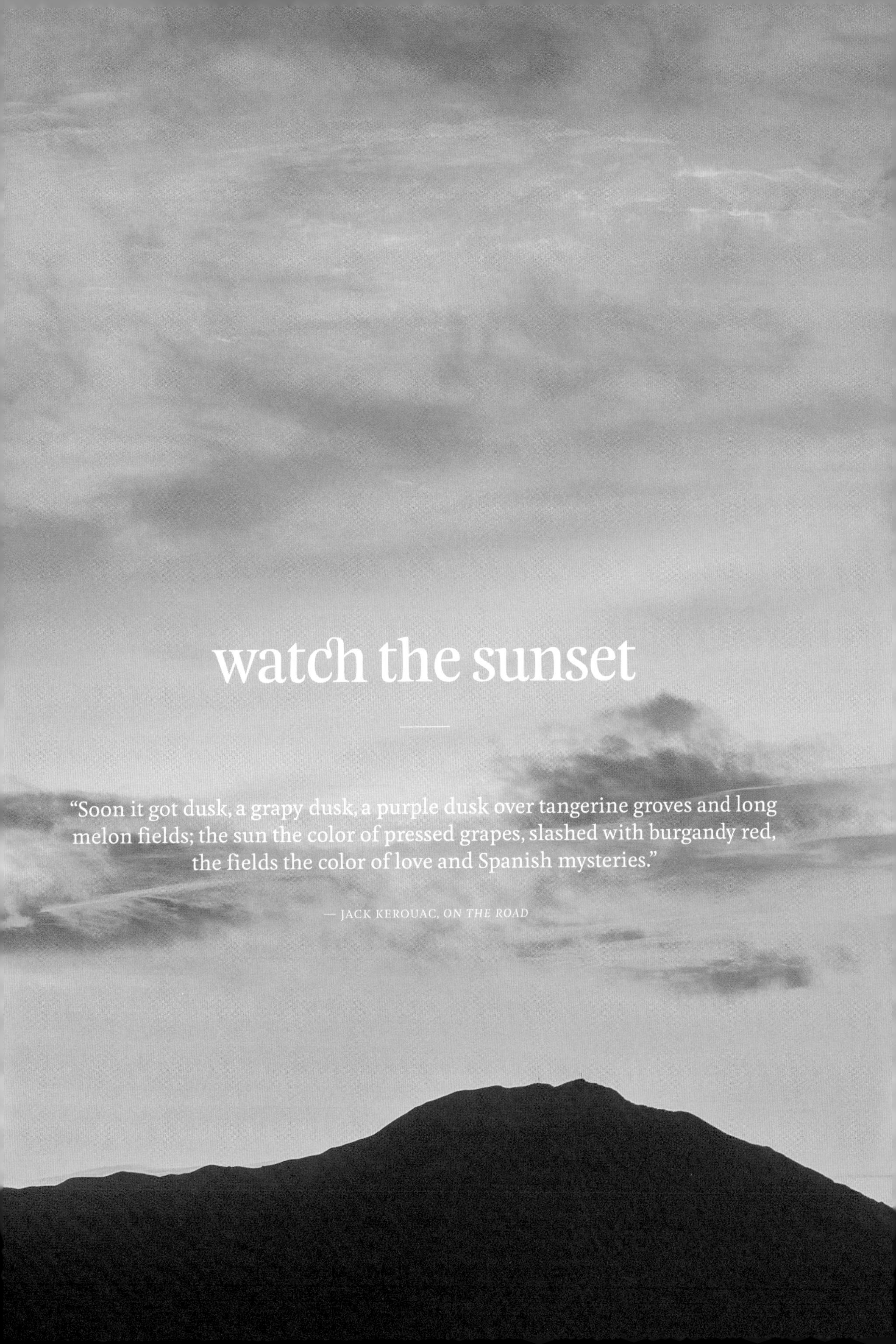

watch the sunset

———

"Soon it got dusk, a grapy dusk, a purple dusk over tangerine groves and long melon fields; the sun the color of pressed grapes, slashed with burgandy red, the fields the color of love and Spanish mysteries."

— JACK KEROUAC, *ON THE ROAD*

NEW MOON
DAY 0

WAXING CRESCENT
DAY 4

FIRST QUARTER
DAY 7

WAXING GIBBOUS
DAY 10

FULL MOON
DAY 14

WANING GIBBOUS
DAY 18

LAST QUARTER
DAY 22

WANING CRESCENT
DAY 26

NEW MOON
DAY 29

Read the moon

The moon is a cold, dry orb studded with craters and strewn with rocks and dust. Its gravitational pull on Earth creates and controls the ocean tides, and it has long held humankind in its dreamy clutches. We mark time by watching its cycles and phases, and even use it for simple navigation.

The moon is the Earth's only satellite. As it circles the Earth, its shape appears to change. Of course, it is not actually changing – this is just how it appears to the human eye, as the moon appears to be different shapes depending on illumination from the sun, and on where the Earth, sun and moon are located in relation to each other.

The changing shapes of the moon are called phases. The moon moves through eight phases in a cycle that lasts 29.5 days, the same amount of time it takes for the Earth to move around the sun.

Waxing moon

The term 'waxing' describes the moon when its illuminated area is increasing. The moon is waxing any time after a new moon and before the full moon.

Waning moon

The term 'waning' describes the moon when its illuminated area is decreasing. The moon is waning any time after a full moon and before the new moon.

Crescent moon

The term 'crescent' is applied to the moon whenever part, but less than half, of its face is illuminated. It sits in the shape of a curved sliver – or crescent, hence the name.

Gibbous moon

When the moon appears more than half lit but less than full it is a gibbous moon. The word gibbous comes from a root word that means hump-backed, and reflects the shape of the moon at this time.

How to navigate using the moon

Navigating by the moon can be a tricky and inexact business, but one quick, simple and easy-to-remember way to get your general bearings is the 'crescent method'. As its name indicates, this moon navigation method can only really be practised around the time of a waxing or waning crescent moon. It's also best done when the moon is high in the sky and not too near the horizon, as the higher the moon is in the sky, the more accurate your reading will be.

To try the method, locate the moon in the sky. Then draw a line in your mind's eye connecting the points (or horns) of the crescent moon, and then extend this line down to the horizon. In the northern hemisphere, the crescent moon method gives an approximate indication of south, and in the southern hemisphere, it gives an approximate indication of north.

gaze at the night sky

"The stars we are given. The constellations we make. That is to say, stars exist in the cosmos, but constellations are the imaginary lines we draw between them, the readings we give the sky, the stories we tell."

— REBECCA SOLNIT, *STORMING THE GATES OF PARADISE: LANDSCAPES FOR POLITICS*

Navigate by the stars

Throughout history, the stars that light up our night skies have been watched and studied by astronomers, and featured in many a myth and legend. Learning to recognize and navigate by the stars is an awe-inspiring and ancient science still practised today by sailors, and you can learn the basics.

You can gaze at the sky for five or 10 minutes and nothing much will happen. But if you sped the night up and watched the sky in fast motion, you'd see plenty of action. You'd see the stars moving across the sky as one. The Earth spins from west to east, so everything in the sky comes into view as we spin towards it and leaves our view as we spin away from it.

To get started with star gazing, wait for the next clear night. Then, choose a location away from streetlights, and take 10–15 minutes to let your eyes adjust to the dark.

Understanding the night sky

Star gazers think about stars as individuals, as asterisms and as constellations.

A star is a luminous sphere of plasma (one of the four fundamental states of matter) held together by its own gravity. The brightest stars have been given proper names. The nearest star to the Earth is the sun. Many others – mostly in the Milky Way galaxy – are visible at night.

An asterism is a recognisable pattern of stars grouped together in a connect-the-dots and stick-figure kind of way. The list of asterisms widely accepted in the Western world can be traced back to Greco-Roman astronomer Claudius Ptolemy, who lived around 1800 years ago. One of the best-known is the Big Dipper, or Plough.

A constellation is a grouping of prominent stars into an area of the celestial sphere, like Andromeda, Perseus and Scorpio. There are 88 officially recognized constellations.

Simple navigation in the northern hemisphere

Polaris, or the North Star, is the one star in the northern night sky that does not appear to move. It sits directly over the North Pole, so once you've found it, you'll always know where north is.

To find the North Star, find the Big Dipper. This group of seven stars is shaped like a saucepan. Three of the stars are in the handle, and four form the pan itself. Next, imagine a line connecting the two stars that form the outer edge of the pan. Continue this line off to the upper right; the first bright star you come to is Polaris, the North Star.

Simple navigation in the southern hemisphere

There is no bright star in the southern sky that can be used to locate due south. Instead, the Southern Cross is used to find the South Celestial Pole.

The Southern Cross is a compact group of bright stars close together in the sky, with two pointer stars always pointing to them from the lower left.

Once you've located the Southern Cross, find the two pointers. Then, use your mind's eye to draw a line perpendicular to the line joining the two pointer stars. The South Celestial Pole is located where that line meets the line formed by the two most widely separated stars in the Southern Cross. From the pole drop a line straight down to the horizon – that's south.

WINTER

walk in the snow

Propagate plants from cuttings

When you propagate plants from cuttings, you're literally cloning the plant; removing a small yet vital part, relocating it and helping it grow anew. Whether it's a delicious fruit tree or a shrub with unique flowers or scent, you can be sure that the next generation of plants will be the same as the original.

GATHER SECATEURS / ROOTING HORMONE OR HONEY (OPTIONAL) / POTS / QUALITY GARDEN SOIL, POTTING MIX OR PROPAGATION MIX / WATERING CAN / LIQUID FERTILIZER

Propagation is the process of creating new plants from seeds, cuttings, roots or bulbs. Cuttings are what you (literally) come away with when you practise the technique of plant cutting – gently cutting away a piece of a source plant's stem or root – or sometimes, just a leaf – and placing it in moist soil, potting or propagation mix. It's also called striking or cloning, and, when successful, will produce new roots and stems, and eventually a whole new plant.

Cuttings can be taken at any time of year. Ideally, cuttings should be taken from firm current season's growth that will comfortably bend 60–90 degrees. Hard, woody material and soft, floppy growth are less likely to succeed – but worth trying, if that's all you've got. It's normal for some cuttings not to take, so don't be disheartened if not all your cuttings flourish into new plants.

Method

1. With clean sharp secateurs, take 10–15 cm (4–6 in) cuttings from the plants you'd like to propagate. Make sure you choose your healthiest-looking plants for parent stock.

2. Gently remove the lower leaves from your cutting, keeping only 4–6 leaves at the top. This helps your new plants direct their energy into creating roots.

3. You can dip the lower 2 cm (⅘ in) of your cutting into rooting hormone gel or powder (available from nurseries) to assist with faster root growth.

Some gardeners also dip their cuttings into honey, which is thought to contain natural rooting agents, and to guard against bacterial or fungal problems.

4. Place your cuttings into a pot with propagation mix or your best garden soil, and gently firm the soil around them. It's fine to place a number of cuttings into the same pot.

5. Water your cuttings well, and place them in a sheltered spot out of direct sunlight. Give them a dose of liquid fertilizer every fortnight or so. If you have a greenhouse, the extra warmth can help your new plants to grow roots more quickly.

6. Put a label on your pot with the date. It can take 4–8 weeks for your plants to develop roots. You'll know your cuttings are doing well when you see new leaves sprouting on their stems. To check the root growth, gently push aside the soil near the base of the stem with a chopstick and take a peek. You can also tug gently on the cuttings – if they don't want to budge, then some roots have grown.

7. Keep your plants moist, and remove any that have died off or succumbed to disease.

8. Once your cuttings have taken root, you can transplant them to a larger pot or directly into your garden.

Bloom branches indoors

Every winter, spring-blooming shrubs and trees do a little groundwork, and set their flower buds. Then, for about six weeks, they go dormant, waiting for spring to ... well, spring, then they get busy again, and blossom. It's possible to coax the buds to bloom early, indoors, for your nature-loving pleasure.

GATHER BRANCHES / SECATEURS, SMALL HANDSAW OR SHARP SCISSORS / HAMMER / WATER / BUCKET OR VASE / SPRAY BOTTLE, FOR MISTING

The technical term for making the flower buds that a tree produces in winter bloom early for the coming spring is 'forcing' – happily, words like 'coaxing', 'nurturing' and 'encouraging' are also fitting descriptions of how you'll go about helping its buds open up early.

Plants and trees suited to forcing include:

- beech
- birch
- buckeye
- cherry
- cornelian dogwood
- crab apple
- flowering almond
- forsythia
- honeysuckle
- lilac
- magnolia
- pussywillow
- quince
- red maple
- redbud
- rhododendron
- spicebush
- spirea
- wisteria
- witch hazel

How to select and cut your branches

Many of the plants in your garden will be suited to blooming indoors. Choose a mild winter day, when branches and their buds will be soft and pliable, and better able to make the transition from cold outdoor temperatures to warm indoor temperatures.

Look for medium-sized branches with plenty of plump flower buds (flower buds are round and fat, while leaf buds are smaller, and pointed). If the buds are just beginning to open, even better.

Cut the branches away from the tree on a diagonal and bruise the cut ends of branches by crushing them with a small hammer so that they'll soak up water faster. For branches thicker than 2 cm (⅘ in) in diameter, use a pair of secateurs or sharp scissors to split the end of the stem by about 4 cm (2 in).

How to prepare branches for forcing

Once you're inside, set the branches in warm water for a few hours. Then, transfer the branches into a vase or bucket of cool water, and move them to a cool place, like a protected porch or garage, where the temperature will stay between 7–12°C (45–55°F). Keep them away from bright, direct sunlight or any direct heat sources, as this will dry them out, and reduce overall bloom color and quality.

Mist the buds frequently with a spray bottle of water, and change the water every few days. Within a few weeks, the buds should begin to unfurl, and the blooms will emerge. Then you can display them in a warm part of the house.

By cutting several branches each week as winter turns to spring, you can have a continual show of color to brighten up your winter months.

Make a dream catcher

The Ojibwa, a Native American and First Nation people of Canada and North America, first made dream catchers to protect their children from bad dreams. Foraging for branches and feathers and making your own dream catcher is a sure way to beautify your bedroom, and sleep easy.

GATHER SUPPLE BRANCHES, LIKE GRAPEVINE, BIRCH, RED WILLOW / CROCHET COTTON, STRING OR WOOL / FEATHERS / SCISSORS / FINE JEWELLERY WIRE / BEADS OR CRYSTALS, FOR THREADING

The legend of the dream catcher

Ojibwa storytellers tell of Asibikaashi, the Spider Woman, who took care of the children and the people on the land. When the Ojibwa Nation spread to the corners of North America it became difficult for Asibikaashi to reach all the children. So she tasked the mothers and grandmothers with weaving magical dream webs, or dream catchers, for the children, using willow hoops and sinew, or cordage made from plants. The dream webs protected the children by catching bad dreams.

How to make your dream catcher

1. Take a few lengths of supple branches and weave them into a loose circular shape. Overlap the ends of the branches and twist them around each other to thicken and strengthen the hoop. Traditionally no wider than an adult's hand, you can make your dream catcher any size your branches will allow.

2. Take your cotton and wind it closely and tightly around the hoop where your branches overlap to reinforce your hoop.

3. To create your web, begin by cutting a 4 m (13 ft) length of cotton. Pick a starting point and loop your cotton around the hoop until you have a small cotton circle – pull the length of the cotton through the circle. This is your first stitch.

4. Pull your cotton 3–5 cm (1–2 in) along the hoop, and then repeat this stitch. Keep going around the hoop until you reach your starting point, pulling each stitch taut, but not too tight.

5. Find the halfway point between your first and second stitch. Loop your cotton over this point. Repeat for every stitch from the first round. This should bend the cotton from the first round towards the centre of the loop. Repeat this method for the third round of stitching, looping your cotton around the midway point between the stitches from the second round. Thread a bead onto the cotton in this round, so you have a 'spider' in the web.

6. Continue your rounds of the hoop until your stitches get to the centre of the hoop. Leave a small circle in the centre of the hoop. To finish, double knot your cotton at the bottom of the circle and cut off any excess thread.

7. Cut a 5 cm (2 in) length of wire, and wind it tightly and closely around the quill end of one of your feathers. Make a small loop at the top end of the wire. Cut a 15 cm (6 in) length of cotton. Thread one end of cotton through the wire loop and wrap it around a few times. Knot it to make sure it's nice and tight. Tie the other end of your length of cotton to the bottom of the hoop, double knotting to secure the feather. Using this method, add as many feathers as you'd like.

8. Cut a 40 cm (16 in) length of thread. Tie each end to two points on opposite sides of your dream catcher, a few centimetres from the uppermost point, to form a loop. Use this loop to hang your dream catcher – and sweet dreams.

Filter air with indoor plants

Filling your living space with leafy green indoor plants isn't just easy on the eye and soothing to the soul; it's good for your health, too. Scientists have proven that particular plants absorb toxic gases through the pores in their leaves, and help to clean and freshen up the air we breathe.

GATHER INDOOR PLANTS / POTTING MIX / POTS / SAUCERS / PEBBLES / LIQUID FERTILIZER

As well as being a welcome pop of green, indoor plants can literally bring fresh air into your midst. When scientists at the National Aeronautics and Space Administration (NASA) started looking for ways to improve the poor air quality in spaceships, they found a simple solution: house plants.

Modern living means that the average house is also susceptible to contaminated air. Gases like carbon dioxide, benzene and formaldehyde can be emitted from common household items, including cosmetics, detergents, plastics, fabrics and furnishings. Luckily, nature's got your back.

Indoor plants can also be edible, calming and colorful, bringing the natural world into your everyday midst and balance to your urban environments. As with all gardens, your indoor plants will thrive best on TLC and soothing music.

Location

In the same way that you decide what plants to grow in your garden based on the amount of space and light available, choose your indoor plants accordingly. Some prefer a shadier spot, others dappled light or full sun. The indoor air temperature and humidity is also important. Some plants need warm air to thrive and others a cooler environment.

It's important to remember that all plants originally come from a particular habitat, climate and place, and the closer you can replicate these conditions indoors, the more your plants will thrive.

Air cleansing power plants

The NASA scientists concluded that nine tropical and subtropical plants, in particular, were air cleansing power plants. This is largely due to the plants' leaf composition, which enables them to photosynthesize well in household light.

Aloe vera is a formaldehyde cleansing plant. Its leaves contain a clear liquid full of vitamins, enzymes, amino acids and other compounds that have wound-healing, antibacterial and anti-inflammatory properties.

Bamboo palm (*Chamardoea seifritzil*) thrives in full sun or bright light and grows as high as 350 cm (138 in). It is fantastic for removing formaldehyde from the air.

Boston fern (*Nephrolepis exaltata v. Bostoniensis*) likes to stay moist, in a cool climate with high humidity and indirect light. It helps to remove formaldehyde and xylene.

Dracaena comes in more than 40 varieties that cleanse your air of benzene, formaldehyde, trichloroethylene and xylene. They all have long, wide leaves, and feature lines of white, cream or red. Pet owners should note they are toxic to cats and dogs.

Weeping fig (*Ficus benjamina*) is a low-maintenance house plant that can grow up to 300 cm (118 in) tall. It likes bright, indirect light and removes benzene, formaldehyde and trichloroethylene.

Garden mum (*Chrysanthemum morifolium*) is the absolute air-cleaning champ. It removes ammonia, benzene, formaldehyde and xylene, and has pretty flowers.

Peace lily (*Spathiphyllum wallisii*) loves shade and can flower all summer long. It removes ammonia, benzene, formaldehyde and trichloroethylene.

Snake plant/Mother-in-law's tongue (*Sansevieria trifasciata*) prefers dry conditions and some direct sun. In fact, it's one of the hardiest house plants around. It helps to remove benzene, formaldehyde, trichloroethylene and xylene.

Spider plant (*Chlorophytum comosum*) is one of the easiest plants to grow indoors. It loves bright indirect sunlight, and will help to remove formaldehyde and xylene from the air.

Care

Always use a potting mix and make sure you have saucers underneath your pots to avoid soil or water damage to furniture or floors. Lining the base of your pots with pebbles keeps your plants healthy by allowing adequate drainage. Your indoor plants require more water over the warmer seasons, and very little in winter. Many indoor plants suffer through excess water rather than too little.

Leaves going brown at the tips can indicate overwatering, and in extreme cases your plants will simply rot and become pest prone.

Indoor plants also get dusty, and this reduces their ability to photosynthesize and purify the air. The easiest way to clean them is to pop them out on a rainy evening, or gently clean the leaves with a water spray bottle and sponge.

Common pests

The most common pests of indoor plants are scale and mealy bugs. Look out for the small brown lumps, or the soft, fuzzy white bodies of mealy bugs. Both pests are sapsuckers, and will gradually weaken the health of your plants. For small infestations it's easiest to pick them off. For larger infestations, you can make your own white oil spray by blending two cups of vegetable oil with one cup of liquid soap, and mixing it until it turns white. Add one tablespoon of the emulsion to one litre of water, shake thoroughly and spray your affected plants. This will suffocate the insects.

Other popular household plants

Other household favorites include potted culinary herbs like parsley, basil and cilantro; succulents, cacti or aloes; hardy perennials like philodendrons, begonias, sansevieria species, bromeliads, colorful crotons and aglaonema species.

Know your knots

To knot, or not to knot? The answer is simple: knot. Knots are one of humankind's most diverse, ancient and useful inventions. They can bear incredible weight, secure incredible loads, and have even inspired a branch of mathematics – knot theory. So what are you waiting for? Get knotting.

GATHER ROPES / A KNIFE

Knowing how to tie a range of basic knots will stand you in good stead for life. Here are a dozen to keep under your belt for those times of need.

Figure eight stopper knot

This is a single-strand knot, made from just one length of rope. It is useful in sailing and rock climbing to stop ropes from running out of retaining devices. It's one of the four basic maritime knots.

Square binding or reef knot

This double-strand knot is good for binding a rope to something, like a post. It is popular with sailors, climbers and gift wrappers. It's also one of the four basic maritime knots.

Overhand stopper knot

A simple single-strand knot that is the beginning of more complicated knots, it's good for tying packages and keeping rope ends from fraying.

Clove hitch knot

This single-strand knot is helpful for securing lines running along a series of posts, belaying, and starting lashings. It's a good knot to use if you want to be able to undo a binding quickly. Also called double hitch, it's another maritime knot.

Gathering wrap knot

A gathering wrap knot is made from just one length of cord. It's used to tie a group of cords together, and is often featured in macrame and other craft projects.

Granny binding knot

A double-strand binding knot used to secure a rope or line around an object. It's similar to a reef knot, but not as strong.

Carrick bend knot

A bend is the name for a knot that joins two ropes together. Used for joining two lines, this knot is especially good for very heavy rope or cable that is too cumbersome for more finely detailed knots.

Cow hitch knot

This is a single-strand knot used to attach a rope to an object. Also called lark's head, deadeye hitch.

Slip knot

This single-strand knot allows you to attach a moveable line to an object, or to bind one end of a rope to the middle of another, and allow the knot to slide along the rope. Also called running knot.

Sheet bend knot

This bend knot can be tied quickly, and is a classic weaver's knot or becket bend.

Fisherman's bend knot

Also called angler's loop, this knot is popular with fishermen. It is very good for joining thin, stiff or slippery lines.

Bowline loop knot

This single-strand knot is used to form a fixed loop at the end of a rope. It's another maritime knot.

FIGURE EIGHT STOPPER KNOT

SQUARE BINDING OR REEF KNOT

OVERHAND STOPPER KNOT

CLOVE HITCH KNOT

GATHERING WRAP KNOT

GRANNY BINDING KNOT

CARRICK BEND KNOT

COW HITCH KNOT

SLIP KNOT

SHEET BEND KNOT

FISHERMAN'S BEND KNOT

BOWLINE LOOP KNOT

Knot a macrame pot hanger

Macrame is an ancient form of textile making based on knotting, rather than weaving or knitting. It originated with 13th century Arab weavers, and was popular with sailors in the 19th century. Its simple system of knots can be turned to almost any purpose, like this pretty but practical pot holder.

GATHER ONE METAL RING (KEYRINGS ARE PERFECT) / FOUR LENGTHS OF FLUORESCENT-COLORED CORD 130 CM (51 IN) / THREE LENGTHS OF FLUORESCENT-COLORED CORD 30 CM (12 IN) / THREE ASSORTED WOODEN BEADS (WITH LARGE CENTRE HOLES) / SMALL GLASS VESSEL

These vibrant hangers are a great beginner's macrame project. Their basic knot design is simple to master, and before long you'll have a stunning feature piece to add to your hanging plant garden. Perfect for small vases and vessels, these colorful pieces make great gifts too.

Method

1. Hook the metal ring onto a nail in the wall, or tape it to a desk. This is the easiest way to work.

2. Thread the four cords through the ring to about halfway along the cords, then fold cords over the ring so you have eight cords in total.

3. Hold a folded piece of cord forming a u-shaped loop against the group of eight cords just underneath the ring, leaving 10 cm (4 in) of excess cord at the top of your loop. Wrap the excess cord around the loop and eight cords four to five times, then push the cord through the bit of loop showing at the bottom of your wrapped cords and pull tight. This will form a gathering knot (see page 195). Trim any excess cord from your knot.

4. Thread all eight cords through the three beads, pushing them up to the base of the wrap knot you just created.

5. Tie another wrap knot below the beads using another 30 cm (12 in) length of cord.

6. Separate your eight cords into bunches of two. Tie an overhand knot with each bunch, about 20 cm (8 in) down from the ring.

7. Group a cord from one bunch with a cord from the next bunch. Knot these together (using overhand knots), around 10 cm (4 in) down from the first set of knots.

8. Separate these new bunches again and repeat Step 5 to form a third row of knots.

9. Tie another wrap knot about 7 cm (3 in) down from the third row of knots to finish, then trim the loose ends of cord to desired length.

10. Fill your small glass vessel with plant cuttings or a little bunch of flowers and slip it inside the hanger to finish.

Grow edible bulbs

Beneath the Earth's surface, where plants put down roots and earthworms dwell, is where root vegetables flourish. It's also the domain of edible bulbs like garlic, onions, fennel and shallots, which are justly revered as culinary essentials.

GATHER KNOBS OF YOUR FAVORITE ORGANIC GARLIC / GOOD QUALITY SOIL / PEA STRAW OR LUCERNE / TROWEL / LIQUID FERTILIZER / COMPOST / WATERING HOSE OR CAN / MULCH

A bulb is the rounded (or bulbous) base of a stem plant. Composed of fleshy, tight, concentric leaf bases, bulbs often have a pungent odour and taste ... because the bulb is actually the stem's food reserves, which enable the plant to survive periods of dormancy. This explains the long gestation period of edible bulbs, which are best planted in winter and harvested six months later, in summer. It also explains their juiciness and concentrated flavor.

Garlic is one of the most popular edible bulbs. Fresh, roasted, smoked, pickled or pureed into paste, garlic is a culinary essential in many kitchens. There are two general varieties of garlic; hardneck (*Allium sativum v. ophioscorodon*) and softneck (*Allium sativum v. sativum*). Hardnecks are better suited to growers in cooler climates, send up strong stalks or 'scapes', and tend to produce fewer but larger cloves. Softnecks suit milder climates, produce bulbs with smaller cloves, mature faster, can be stored longer than hardneck varieties, and are easily braided.

Garlic can be sown from mid-fall to mid-winter. Folk wisdom suggests planting on the shortest day, the winter solstice, and harvesting on the longest, the summer solstice. Choose quality organic garlic from your local greengrocer, farmers' market or a local nursery, or obtain bulbs from a friend's garden.

Growing garlic

1. Find a sunny spot in your garden, with a depth of at least 20 cm (8 in) of good quality soil. Garlic can grow in most soils, but you'll get a better crop from well-composted and manured soil. If you're short on space, you can also grow your garlic in a deep pot.

2. Break your garlic heads into individual cloves, and plant each clove 20 cm (8 in) apart with the pointed tip up, an inch below the soil surface.

3. Give your newly planted garlic cloves a good soak, and mulch them with pea straw or lucerne. They benefit from plenty of sun and nutrients, and regular, deep watering.

4. Continue to feed your garlic cloves with liquid fertilizer and handfuls of compost or aged manures every 4–6 weeks.

5. It takes roughly 5–6 months for your garlic to mature. You'll know it's ready when the stems start to wilt and go soft at the base. You can also gently scrape back the soil around your garlic heads to check the size of your cloves. To harvest, carefully pull your garlic up then brush off the soil and store in a dry, cool, well-ventilated spot in your home or garage. Garlic can also be hung in bunches or placed as separate heads in a newspaper-lined box.

Remember to keep some of the best heads for next season's planting.

Parsnip and apple soup with tarragon and parsnip crisps

You can never have enough winter soups in your repertoire – they are warming, nourishing, and use up bulk winter produce. Apples bring some sweetness and tang to lift the parsnips, the roasted garlic adds extra depth, and the subtle anise flavors of tarragon bring aromatic flavor to the soup.

SERVES 6

Tarragon oil, tarragon and walnut relish

MAKES ABOUT ½ CUP OIL, ABOUT 1 CUP RELISH

45 g (1½ oz) tarragon

125 ml (¾ cup/4½ fl oz) olive oil
+ 80 ml (⅓ cup/3 fl oz) for drizzling

160 g (1¼ cups/5½ oz) walnuts, toasted*

20 g (⅘ oz) parsley

1 teaspoon lemon juice

salt + pepper

Crispy parsnip chips

250 g (9 oz) parsnips, scrubbed and patted dry

2 tablespoons oil

salt

Tarragon oil, tarragon and walnut relish

1. Blend the tarragon and 125 ml oil to a puree. Transfer to a small saucepan over a medium-low heat and cook for 3 minutes to release the flavors.

2. Drain off 2 tablespoons of the oil and set aside for serving.

3. In a food processor, combine the remaining tarragon puree, walnuts, parsley, lemon juice and ¼ teaspoon salt. Blend to a rough puree.

Crispy parsnip chips

1. Preheat oven to 200°C (400°F) and line a large roasting tray with baking paper.

2. Using a potato peeler, peel the parsnips into thin strips. Combine parsnip strips, oil and a sprinkling of salt and lay over the baking tray in a single layer.

3. Bake for about 20 minutes until crisp, turning after 10 minutes.

*Walnuts can be toasted in a saucepan over a medium heat on the stovetop and cooked on each side for about 2–3 minutes. They can also be toasted in an oven spread out on a tray lined with baking paper at 190°C (375°F) for about 5–10 minutes, stirring occasionally to ensure even cooking.

Note: Tarragon also has a beautiful bright yellow flower before it goes to seed, which can be used to pretty up dishes when serving.

Roasted garlic, parsnip and apple soup

1 head garlic (about 10 cloves)

60 g (2 oz) butter

2 leeks

2 celery sticks

2 sweet apples

1 bay leaf

125 ml (½ cup/4 fl oz) dry white wine

750 g (26 oz) parsnips, peeled and cut into 1 cm pieces

750 ml (3 cups/26 fl oz) vegetable stock

salt + freshly ground white pepper

Roasted garlic, parsnip and apple soup

1. Preheat oven to 200°C (400°F).

2. Cut the top off the head of garlic and discard. Drizzle the remainder with olive oil, wrap in foil and roast for about 30 minutes, until soft.

3. In a large saucepan, combine butter, leeks and celery over a medium heat. Stir until butter has melted and mix well to combine, then cover, reduce heat to low and sweat for 7 minutes. Add apples and bay leaves and sweat for another 3 minutes. Add the wine, increase heat to high and cook for 1 minute.

4. Add chopped parsnips and roasted garlic and mix together. Pour in stock and 750 ml water. Cover and bring to the boil, then reduce heat to medium-low and simmer for 15 minutes.

5. Remove bay leaves, transfer to a blender or food processor, or use a stick blender to blend until smooth.

6. Return to the pan, add water if you prefer a thinner soup, and salt and white pepper to taste.

7. Serve the soup with the tarragon relish stirred through, a drizzle of oil and sprinkle of crisps.

Grow mushrooms

Animal, vegetable, mineral ... or fungus? Mushrooms are lords of their own classificatory kingdom – the Fungi Kingdom – and unlike most edible plants, these other-worldly victuals grow in the dark. And once they get started, boy, they can really mushroom, as much as doubling their size in 24 hours.

GATHER MUSHROOM KIT / SPRAY BOTTLE / WATER

Mushrooms are the fruiting bodies of a fungus known as mycelium. They grow from spores – not seeds – that are so tiny you can't see them with the naked eye.

Each mushroom has roughly 16 billion spores on its gills, the fluted brown underside of the mushroom cap. Because the spores don't contain chlorophyll, which normally kickstarts germination (as seeds do), spores rely on substances like grain, sawdust, straw, wood chips, liquid and even coffee grounds for nourishment. A blend of the spores and these nutrients is called spawn, which acts a bit like a yogurt culture or sourdough bread starter.

The spawn itself could grow mushrooms, but you'll get a better mushroom harvest by applying the spawn to a substrate. Depending on the mushroom type, the substrate could be straw, cardboard, logs, wood chips, or compost with a blend of materials like straw, corncobs, cotton and cocoa seed hulls, gypsum and nitrogen supplements.

The spawn supports the growth of the mushrooms' tiny, white, threadlike roots – that's the mycelium. These grow first, before the mushroom itself pushes through the substrate or growing medium.

Growing mushrooms

As a beginner, the easiest way to start growing mushrooms is to purchase a kit from your local nursery. All you'll need to do is keep your kit moist, and in a cool dark place in your home.

Mushroom kits are also great for people who live in smaller homes or apartments. Make sure your kit is white with mycelium growth before you open the plastic cover, and spread the peat moss casing material on top. If it's still brown you'll need to close it up and leave it for a few days to a week and check again.

Varieties you can explore growing at home include white button, portobello, oyster, shitake and enoki.

Mushrooms thrive in dark, cool, moist and humid environments. In a home, a garage is often ideal, but a dedicated spot under a sink or in a cupboard may be all you need.

Most mushrooms grow best in temperatures between 17–20°C (60–70°F). Some, like enoki mushrooms, prefer cooler temperatures, so growing them inside in winter works well.

It takes roughly 3–5 weeks for your first crop of mushrooms to flourish. Gently harvest each mushroom so that you do not disturb the remaining mushrooms. You'll normally get two good crops from your kit, and then a few last mushrooms as your mycelium dies. Once your kit has finished fruiting you can add it to your compost or dig it directly into your garden beds.

Make string and cordage

Making string, cordage and ropes from plant fibres is an ancient art. This simple 2-ply cordage is a pleasure to make, creates tight and even string of very high quality, and can be used for all sorts of projects, from jewelry making and gift wrapping to basket making, net weaving and bush craft adventures.

GATHER PLANT FIBRES / WATER

Stinging nettle, reeds, rushes and grasses, barks and even animal hair can all be used to make strings, cords and ropes. Rushes, reeds and grasses are easy to begin with, as you can use them straight from the plant. Use fibres of similar thickness – this is key to making good, strong cord.

Preparing your fibres

Dampen your fibres with water to make them supple and easier to grip. Some fibres are suited to soaking, others to dunking, and others to simply having water run over them with wet fingers. Experiment with a sample fibre to work out what suits your fibres best.

If you have a range of fibres of varying thickness, group them together according to thickness, and use them to make separate strings. Of course, all strands vary and thin out at some point; don't worry too much about this, as you'll add a new fibre in at the point where a strand starts to thin.

Making an eye

Always begin by making an 'eye': a loop for the end. To do this, take up two lengths of fibre and stagger them so that the ends are uneven. This is so when the ends run short later they don't end (and therefore need to have new fibre woven in) at the same time.

Now locate the area where the two lengths are overlapping. Pinch the centre of this area between your thumb and forefinger, then meet it with the other thumb and forefinger, and start to twist the fibres in opposite directions. As tension builds the fibres will naturally kink to form a small eye; this is the very first twist at the beginning of your cord.

Weaving fibres into cordage

Pinch and hold the fibres at the eye, so that your two lengths of fibre are parallel. Then, take the strand that is furthest away from you with your other thumb and forefinger, and twist it tightly. Maintaining the tautness in that twist, bring the strand forward, crossing it over the top of the strand that is closest to you, so that the strands swap places. Move your hold along the cord to just above where the two strands separate. Repeat the process of taking the strand that is furthest away from you, twisting it and holding it taut, then crossing it up and over the front strand. And so on, until you feel that one of the two strands is becoming thinner than the other, which signals that it's time to add in a new strand of the fibre. Take a new fibre of suitable thickness and add the end in, on top of the thinner strand, at the point where the two strands in your existing cord meet. Pinch it into place, then carry on twisting and rolling your cord (and adding in new fibres, as needed) until you have the length you desire.

211

Make a string bag

Archaeologists have discovered fragments of bags and nets made with knotless netting in ancient civilizations from Scandinavia to America, so you can be sure that by following these steps you are creating a bag that will stand the test of time. You'll need a bag to take on your adventures – why not make one yourself?

GATHER MATERIALS TO MAKE CORDAGE OR PRE-MADE STRING / A BLUNT TAPESTRY NEEDLE / SCISSORS

Once you've mastered making your own cordage (see previous page), follow these simple steps to turn your string into something that will give you pleasure every time you use it – a string bag.

Method

1. Find a comfortable sitting position, then take several metres of string or cordage and wrap it twice around your thigh, or around both legs if you want to make a large bag. Tie a knot at one end of the string. This will be the rim of your bag.

2. Find the other end of string and thread it through a blunt tapestry needle.

3. Point your needle over the rim and pull down on the end until you have a small loop under the rim. You can make this loop as big or small as you like – this will determine the size of the gaps in your bag.

4. Then point the string back through the front of the nearest side of the loop and pull it tight so you have created a twist.

5. Repeat this stitch along the row, turning it around your leg as you go until you have loops all the way along the string as it circles your legs.

6. The first stitch in the second row is created by pointing your needle through the very lowest part of the loop in the row above.

7. Carry on stitching rows of loops in this way until the bag is as long as you want it to be.

8. When you are finished, slip the bag down your leg.

9. For a square bottom simply lie the bag flat and do a row of running stitch in and out of the loops joining them together

10. For a round bottom skip stitches in each row until the bottom is just one tight loop and stitch the final row together.

11. Finish with a knot and trim any messy bits with scissors.

12. To make a simple handle, run a piece of cordage under the rim and twist or plait it together and tie it off on the other side.

Tip: for a neat look it is important to keep your loops consistent in size and keep checking the shape of your bag.

nest

"Nature is not a place to visit. It is home."

— GARY SNYDER, *THE PRACTICE OF THE WILD*

Extract dyes from plants

Before there were synthetic dyes coloring our world, there was nature. People have been working with dyes made from plants for thousands of years, and the process for extracting pigments from plants and using them to color wool, cotton and silk has changed little over time.

GATHER RUBBER GLOVES / DRIED OR FRESH PLANT MATTER / LARGE POT / WATER / COLANDER / LARGE BOWL OR SECOND POT / FABRIC / LARGE SPOON / TOWEL

Plants and colors

Dye can be extracted from dried plant materials, like roots and hardwood chips, or from fresh plant materials, like roots, leaves and flowers.

You can experiment with any plant to see what color you can draw from it. Here are some plants that are commonly used for dyeing:

- Blue – red cabbage, blueberries, blackberries
- Green – nettle, spinach
- Orange – yellow onion, dandelion heads
- Purple – elderberries, mulberries
- Pink – strawberries, cherries, roses
- Red – hibiscus or sumac flowers
- Yellow – dandelion, marigold, daffodil, and goldenrod flowers

Safety notes

Always wear rubber gloves when handling dyes, dyed fabrics and mordants, and never use your gloves, dye vessels or spoons for cooking.

Extracting and preparing the dye

To extract dye from dried materials, cut your material into small pieces and put them in a pot. Then cover them with warm water and soak them overnight. The next day, add more water, then put the pot on the stove. Bring the mixture to a boil then reduce it to a simmer. Keep it simmering for at least half an hour, bearing in mind that the color will be lighter once it has dried on the fabric you

dye, so it needs to look darker than your desired end color. When the color looks good, strain the liquid through a colander into a heat resistant pot or bowl. This is the dye.

To extract dye from fresh materials, follow the steps outlined for extracting dye from dried materials, except for the overnight soaking – the pot can go on the stove straight away. After the dye has been strained, your dye bath is ready.

Note that you can use your dye mixture for several dyeing sessions. It can be drained, cooled and re-used immediately, or stored in the fridge, until it goes mouldy.

Fabrics suited to dyeing

Wool, cotton and silk are all able to take natural dyes. To get the best results, treat them with a mordant first – that's a compound, typically an inorganic oxide, that will fix the color.

Dyeing fabric

When you are ready to dye your fabric, wet it with a quick submerge, then place it in the dye bath. Let it simmer on the stove for about 30 minutes – or until it is the desired color (the longer you leave it in the dye bath, the deeper the color). Gently stir it from time to time to ensure the color is distributed evenly. After 30 minutes, or when you are satisfied with the color, drain the dye through the colander again. Rinse the fabric well in cool water before laying it on a towel to dry.

Felt balls

Felt is a textile made by matting, condensing and pressing fibres together. It is used from fashion, to building, to car design. These felt balls are made from wool, and can be used in jewelry making, strung and hung, or even used as indoor bouncy balls - yes, they really bounce!

GATHER FELTING WOOL OR FLEECE / RUBBER GLOVES / JUG OF HOT SOAPY WATER / JUG OF PLAIN HOT WATER / TOWEL / TOOTHPICKS, CRAFT NEEDLES OR KNITTING NEEDLES (OPTIONAL) / BAKING TRAY

Gather as many different wisps of vibrantly colored felting wool or fleece together as you can. You can also work in scraps of natural yarn. Your local craft shop will have plenty of variety.

If you are dyeing your own wool (see previous page), make sure the wool has been fully dried from the dyeing process. Gently pull and stretch the wool into wisps with your hands before you get started, and wear gloves while making your ball.

Making a felt ball

Begin with a small wad of wool, then wrap lengths of wool tightly around it. Keep adding layers until it is roughly twice the size you want it to be when you're done.

Next, saturate the wool in the jug of hot, soapy water, then gently pass it from hand to hand, rolling it to shape into a ball, without squeezing. Work over the top of a bath towel, to soak up any water that drops as you're working. Do this for about 10 minutes, dipping the ball in the plain hot water if the ball cools down. Don't worry if it doesn't look quite like a ball just yet. That will come.

Adding designs

Spots and stripes are both easy additions to make to your felt ball. To make spots, wind a small wisp of wool into a rough ball shape, poke it into the larger ball with a toothpick or knitting needle, dip it in the water, and keep rolling the ball.

To make stripes, work strips of wool into the ball with your fingertips, dip it, and keep rolling.

Finishing the ball

Keep rolling the ball in your palms some more, dipping it in the hot soapy water again if it cools. If it gets too soapy, dip and rinse it in the jug of plain hot water, squeeze it, and continue rolling and shaping it.

The more you roll, the smaller and denser the ball will get – this is when it really starts to take shape, and when you can apply more pressure to achieve a round ball shape.

If you plan to use the balls for jewelry making or stringing, take a toothpick or knitting needle and push a hole through it while it's still wet, then give it a final roll.

When the ball has shrunk and condensed to the size you desire, rinse it with cool water, place it on the baking tray, and let dry.

If it is misshapen or has a 'crack' in it (where the fibres have not melded together), simply take a jar or other flat weight and thump the ball around a bit, to mash the fibres together, then roll it again.

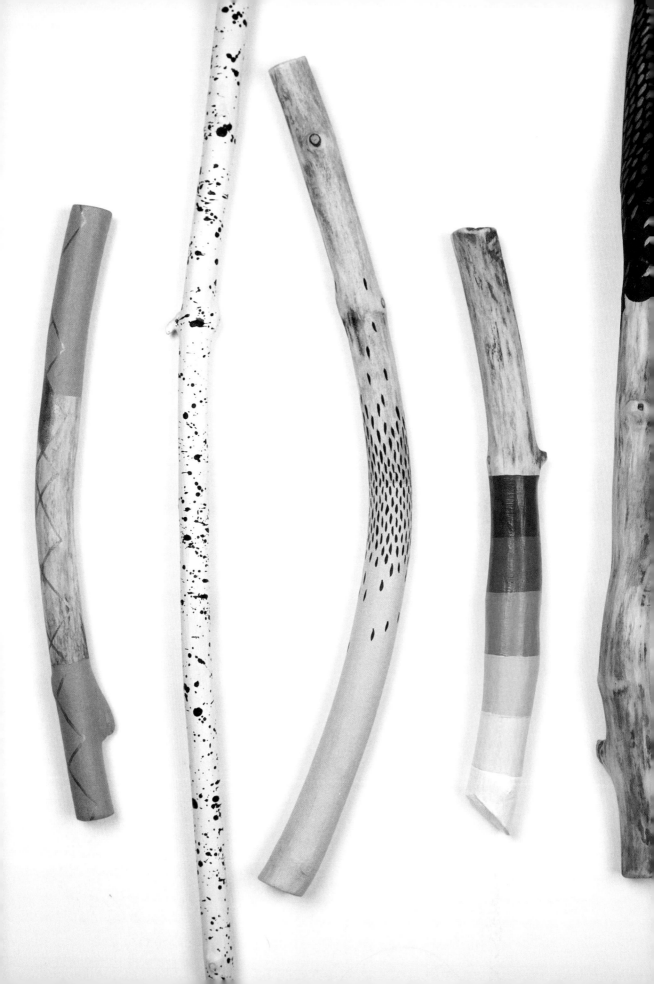

Paint sticks

Five, six, pick up sticks. On one of your rambles outdoors,
keep a hawk eye out for an interesting stick to take home and
turn into beautiful - and sustainable - art. It's a simple, soothing
project; not like your childhood game at all.

GATHER SANDPAPER / ACRYLIC PAINT OR ACRYLIC INK / BRUSHES (VARYING SIZES) / STICKS

Pick up sticks

A walk through the park or along the waterfront
will uncover sticks just dying to be decorated. Look
for sticks with some personality, craggy knots or a
funny bend. Straight ones are easiest to decorate,
and also to hang once finished.

Prepare and decorate your stick

Clean your stick thoroughly in soapy water and set
aside to dry. Once the stick is bone dry, sand the
surface until nice and smooth.

Use acrylic paint for this project – you can also
use some primer to prep the base if you have some
handy. You don't need to start with a plan for your
decoration. Simply apply a base color and then
have fun with your paint, creating bands of color,
adding polka dots, zig zags or other patterns.
Take a sketchpad along with you when you go
rambling and draw some of the patterns you find
in nature – these will look fantastic translated
into vibrant color on one of your sticks.

Once your paint has dried, apply a layer of varnish
(use one designed for acrylic paint) and let it dry.

Display your painted stick

A collection of sticks looks great hanging on a
wall, either over a headboard or on a large wall.
Your sticks will need to be relatively straight to be
mounted to a wall. Why not use your more curvy
sticks in a forage hanging (see page 53)?

Lean your sticks against walls and tuck them into
corners around the house. When you stumble across
them, it will remind you of your walk in nature –
and might just inspire you to take another one.

Build a campfire

Fire is one of nature's most powerful forces, and an essential part of the human experience. A campfire provides warmth and light, protection from wild animals, and a means of cooking food. It can inspire storytelling, soul baring, romance and camaraderie.

GATHER TINDER / KINDLING / FUEL WOOD / MATCHES / BUCKET OF WATER

Building, lighting and managing fires is a serious undertaking. Make sure you only light fires in permitted areas and at permitted times, and keep a bucket of water handy. Never leave a fire unattended and make sure it's completely out before you leave a site.

Create a fire bed

If your campsite has a designated fire area, use it. Otherwise, you'll need to make your own. Select an area away from trees, bushes, and other plant material. Your fire bed should be on bare earth, not grass (especially not dead grass).

Now it's time to make your fire bed. Use your hands, a stick or a spade to gather dirt into a mound in the centre of your cleared area. The mound should be 8–10 cm (3–4 in) thick.

Gather your wood

Check with your campsite authorities first as some require you to take your own wood or purchase theirs. You'll need three basic materials to build your campfire: tinder, kindling, and fuel wood (all deadwood gathered from the ground). You'll add them to the fire in this order, too.

Tinder – a good campfire starts with a generous clutch of dry leaves, bark, wood shavings and dry grass, about the size of a large pinecone.

Kindling – this consists of dry twigs and branches ranging in thickness. The thickest pieces should be about the width of a pencil. Kindling is the mediator of the fire building world – tinder burns fast but is

relatively volatile; if you throw fuel wood on straight away, you'll suffocate it. Kindling helps your fire grow big and strong, and readies it for the fuel wood.

Fuel wood – Dry branches roughly the width of your arm are the best wood to use to really get your fire burning. Big logs are okay too, but save them for when the fire is well established.

The type of fire you want will depend on what you plan to do with it. Here are three of the most common fire builds, and what they're suited to.

Snack fire

This fire is good for brewing coffee or frying up a snack, and is sometimes called a teepee fire. It is quick to build and easy to clean, so it's also good if you're not staying in one spot for long.

Start by placing your tinder bundle in the middle of your fire bed. Next, form a teepee above your tinder bundle. Use the thinnest pieces of kindling, and be sure to leave an opening in the teepee on the side the wind is blowing against. This will ensure that your fire gets the air it needs, and will blow the flames onto the kindling.

Continue adding kindling to the teepee, working your way up to pencil-sized twigs. Then, create a larger teepee structure around your kindling teepee with your fuel wood.

Finally, place a match under your tinder. Because this set-up directs the flame up, the flame should start under the tinder, then rise to the kindling and then on to the fuel wood. The teepee structure will eventually fall. When this happens, simply add more fuel logs to the fire.

Cooking fire

A cooking fire acts as a natural cooking range. It lets you arrange an exclusive spot for your camping kettle and pots and pans – one just beside or above the flames (which means that your food and your pots won't burn). It's the type of fire you want to build if you plan to stay at a campsite for a few days, and cook and eat delicious food while you're there.

Line up all the cooking gear you'll want to suspend over the fire, then find two green logs that are long enough to encompass all of your gear. These logs will serve as the edges of your cooking range, so it's important that they're the right size. Lay them aside while you build your fire.

Then, build a large snack fire. When it's burning nicely, lay the two green logs either side of it, about 18 cm (7 in) apart at one end, and 10 cm (4 in) at the other. Smaller vessels like kettles and coffee pots can go on the narrower end, and larger pots and pans can go on the wider end.

If your pots have rungs or a handle, you can suspend them over the fire. To do this, find two sturdy forked logs about two feet tall and insert them into the ground at either end of the fire with the forks pointing up. Next, find a strong, straight stick. Hang your pots from it, then run it between the forks above the fire.

Keep your cooking fire burning all the time so you have an ample supply of coals. You can spread or pile the coals to create hotter or cooler cooking areas.

Comfort fire

This beauty provides hours of cosiness by channelling all the warmth of the fire in one direction. It's perfect when camping under the stars on cold nights.

The comfort fire is also called a reflector fire, and that's exactly how it works. Building a simple backdrop behind the fire stops it from throwing heat off in all directions, reflecting it away from itself (and at you) instead.

Try to find a natural reflector – something incombustible – to build your fire in front of. A cliff, large rock, or earth bank will work.

If you can't find a natural reflector, build your own by driving two hearty stakes into the ground at an angle behind where you'll lay your fire.

Against these slanted poles, stack a row of logs from largest at the bottom to smallest at the top, to form a backstop that will serve as the reflector. Use only green wood so it won't burn.

Next, build a snack fire about a foot away from it then light it up, settle in and enjoy its warmth.

How to put a fire out

Stop adding wood to your fire, and wait for the wood that is already on the fire to burn completely to ash. Take your bucket of water, and pour water onto the fire (if you don't have any water you can use dirt or sand). When the fire comes into contact with the water it will make a hissing sound; keep pouring until the hissing stops. Then, stir the ashes and embers with a shovel. Make sure everything is wet and that the ashes and embers are cold to the touch.

Poppyseed campfire bread with rhubarb compote

This recipe for unleavened bread can be cooked wrapped in foil or inside a cast-iron pot and popped into the coals of a fire, or wrapped around sticks and held over coals. It's a camping favorite when served hot, laden with butter, syrups and jams.

SERVES 6-8

Poppyseed campfire bread

450 g (3 cups/16 oz) self-raising flour

½ teaspoon salt

60 g (2 oz) butter, plus extra to serve

40 g (¼ cup/1½ oz) poppyseeds

125 ml (½ cup/4 fl oz) milk

Rhubarb, honey and earl grey compote

500 g (18 oz) rhubarb, cut into ½ cm (¼ inch) pieces

2 teaspoons honey

125 ml (½ cup/4 fl oz) strongly brewed earl grey tea

50 g (¼ cup/1½ oz) sugar

Poppyseed campfire bread

1. Find sticks at least 1.5 cm (½ in) in width, strong enough to hold dough wrapped around it. Wash and dry the sticks thoroughly.

2. Combine flour and salt in a large mixing bowl. Rub in the butter to resemble breadcrumbs, then mix in the poppyseeds. Create a well in the middle and add milk and ½–¾ cup water. Mix the flour into the liquid and bring the mixture together to form a dough.

3. Divide dough into portions and roll into logs no wider than 2 cm (⅘ in) and wrap around sticks.

4. Once the fire has burnt to embers, place your campfire bread stick over the embers and cook until it sounds hollow when you tap it, around 10–15 minutes depending on the heat of the fire and the width of the dough.

5. You can also bake the campfire bread in an oven at 200°C (400°F) for 20–30 minutes.

Rhubarb, honey and earl grey compote

1. Combine all ingredients in a saucepan over a medium heat and simmer for 10–15 minutes, until thickened.

To serve

Serve campfire bread with butter and rhubarb compote and a hot cup of tea.

look out

Thank you

A sincere thank you to the community of people that were part of the
creation of *Connect with Nature*. The idea of doing a book on connecting with
nature through projects and activities evolved through numerous chats with
friends, family, bike rides and cups of tea. Thanks to Eliza Edwards, Liz Ginis and
Melissa Kayser who helped me develop the idea from the beginning.

Thank you to Kasia Pawlikowski my colleague and lady of many talents.
She never ceases to inspire me with her design, intelligence and commitment
to making this book – the results speak for themselves.

Thank you to all the contributors: writers, makers, artists, photographers
who brought this book to life and shared their talents so generously.

Thank you to Hardie Grant and our lovely editor Lauren Whybrow
who have believed in this book since the beginning.

Thank you to all the organisations who have worked with Viola Design since
1999 and shared our vision for making this planet a more beautiful place.

Lastly, thanks to my family Nick, Tasman, Freya, Diana and Chris
and their unwavering support. And all my friends,
you know who you are – thank you.

Acknowledgements

Art direction and design

Anna Carlile
Kasia Pawlikowski
www.violadesign.com.au

Writers

Vanessa Murray
www.vanessa-murray.com

Amadis Lacheta
www.amadislacheta.com

Jessica Thompson
Liz Ginis
Bayden Packwood Hine
Natasha Newton
Kitiya Palaskas
Harriet Goodall
Courtney Wotherspoon

Recipes

Jessica Thompson
www.palate-journal.com

Makers

Wildflower wreath and tussie mussie
Wona Bae
www.looseleafstore.com.au

Forage wall hanging
Eliza Edwards

Terrarium
Charlotte Nicdao
Bayden Packwood Hine
www.plantbypackwood.com

Painted stones
Natasha Newton
www.natasha-newton.co.uk

Pinch pots
Kasia Pawlikowski
Valerie Restarick

Dream catcher
Stina Johansson

Macrame pot hangers
Kitiya Palaskas
www.kitiyapalaskas.com

Cordage and string bag
Harriet Goodall
www.harrietgoodall.com

Painted sticks
Courtney Wotherspoon
www.spoonstudio.com

Photography

Anna Carlile
www.violadesign.com.au
Cover, stones and wreath
Spring, 2–3
Farro salad with spring greens, 12
Raise plants from seed, 14
Keep chickens, 18, 21
Hail the honeybee, 25
Sprout seeds and beans, 26
Energy balls, 32
Weave a wreath of wildflowers, 36
Make a pocket press, 40
Mix seed bombs, 48
Forage and create a wall hanging, 52, 54–55
Grow herbs, 74
Make herbal teas, 76
Make a tussie mussie, 78, 80–81
Make scented mists and sprays, 85
Heirloom tomato and peach salad, 90
Paint stones, 98, 100, 101
Blueberry and spelt galette, 104, 106–107
Attract birds, 126
Preserve abundance, 137
Buckwheat crepes, 138, 140–141
Beet gnocchi with nettle pesto, 146, 149
Make a kite, 154
Pinch pots, 158
Print leaves, 164
Propagate plants from cuttings, 182
Make a dream catcher, 186
Filter air with indoor plants, 188, 192, 193
Knot a macrame pot hanger, 198
Parsnip and apple soup, 202, 205
Make string and cordage, 210
Make a string bag, 212, 214, 215
Felt balls, 222
Paint sticks, 224
Poppyseed campfire bread with rhubarb compote, 232
Thank you, 236

Emilie Ristevski
www.helloemilie.com
Cover, mushrooms
Spreads, 34–35, 38–39, 170–171,
Gaze at the night sky, 172–173
Grow mushrooms, 208
Nest, 216

Jason Charles Hill
www.jasoncharleshill.com
Spreads, 56–57, 226–227
Walk in nature, 28–29
Navigate by the stars, 174
Walk in the snow, 178

Johan Lolos
www.johanlolos.com
Spreads, 72–73, 160–161, 162–163, 180–181, 206–207
Waldeinsamkeit, 110–111
Watch the sunset, 166–167
Look out, 234–235

Marta Potoczek
www.martapotoczek.com
Cover, nettles
Start a veggie patch, 6, 9, 10, 11
Grow heirloom tomatoes, 88
Forage for edible weeds, 144

Megan Robinson
www.meganrobinsonblog.com
Go on a picnic, 108–109

Teagan Glenane
www.teaganglenane.com.au
Create a terrarium, 92, 94–95

Unsplash
www.unsplash.com
Paul Jarvis, inside cover
Jan Erik Waider, introduction
Jonas Nilsson Lee, 4–5
Bryan Rodriquez, 30
Jacob Aguilar-Friend, 31
Alexander Shustov, 44–45, 152
Chris Sardegna, 46, 60
Charles Yeager, 51
Sebastien Gabriel, 58–59
Susanne Feldt, 62–63
Aleksandra Boguslawska, 82–83
Jeremy Cai, 96–97
Iswanto Arif, 114–115
Wilson Lau, 118–119
Roger Burkhard, 124–125
Jennifer Trovato, 128–129
Veronika Sulinská, 132
Jordan Sanchez, 142–143
Alex Jones, 156
Taylor Leopold, 176–177

Shutterstock
www.shutterstock.com
Voronina Svetlana, 16
Mimage Photography, 42
Plamen, 68
Mythja, 71
Piotr Marcinski, 112
Mona Makela, 130
Casanisa, 134
Sunny Forest, 150–151
David Carillet, 168
Iravgustin, 184
Sukiyaki, 190–191
Fotografiche, 194
Artistas, 200
Akiyoko, 217
Ostill, 220
SSokolov, 231

iStock by Getty Images
www.istockphoto.com
Darios44, 22
Bunhill, Tapsiful, Amit erez, 64
Goldfinch photography, Olada, 67
Vitaliy_87, 102
Karnauhov, 103

Getty Images
www.gettyimages.com.au
David Trood, 50

Nanamee
www.nanamee.com
Bernd Vonau, 153

Ian Jacobs, 64
Hehaden, Peter Visser, 67
Michael Paul Young, 122

Props

Trowel on cover by Grafa
www.grafa.com.au

Ceramics

Kim Wallace
www.kwceramics.com.au

Valerie Restarick
www.valerierestarick.com

Locations

Keep chickens and propagate plants from cuttings, Ceres Environment Park

Knot a macrame pot hanger, Crowley/Cornhill residence

Indoor plants, Looseleaf

The publisher would like to acknowledge the following individuals and organisations:

Editorial manager
Melissa Kayser

Project editor
Lauren Whybrow

Editor
Alice Barker

Writers
Vanessa Murray, Amadis Lacheta,
Jessica Thompson, Liz Ginis

Art direction and design
Anna Carlile, Kasia Pawlikowski, Viola Design

Pre-press
Splitting Image

The author gratefully acknowledges permission to reprint excerpts from the below titles.

An Aperture Monograph on Paul Caponigro by Paul Caponigro, reproduced by permission of Aperture. All rights reserved.

Bluebeard's Egg by Margaret Atwood, copyright © 1983 O.W. Toad Ltd, reproduced by permission of Houghton Mifflin Harcourt Publishing Company. All rights reserved.

By-Line by Ernest Hemingway, published by Arrow, reproduced by permission of The Random House Group Ltd. All rights reserved.

On The Road by Jack Kerouac, copyright © John Sampas Lit. Rep., reproduced by permission of SLL/Sterling Lord Literistic, Inc. All rights reserved.

Storming the Gates of Paradise: Landscapes for Politics by Rebecca Solnit, copyright © 2007 The Regents of the University of California, reproduced by permission of University of California Press. All rights reserved.

The Practice of the Wild by Gary Snyder, copyright © 1990, reproduced by permission of Counterpoint. All rights reserved.

"Rising and Falling: The Theorists of Bipedalism", from Wanderlust: A History of Walking by Rebecca Solnit, copyright © 2000 by Rebecca Solnit, reproduced by permission of Viking Books, an imprint of Penguin Publishing Group, a division of Penguin Random House LLC.

The author gratefully acknowledges Professor Edward O. Wilson of Harvard University for his assistance and for granting permission.

Explore Australia Publishing Pty Ltd
Ground Floor, Building 1, 658 Church Street
Richmond, VIC 3121

Explore Australia Publishing Pty Ltd is a division of Hardie Grant Publishing Pty Ltd

hardie grant publishing

Published by Explore Australia Publishing Pty Ltd, 2016

Form © Explore Australia Publishing Pty Ltd, 2016

Design, images and text © Anna Carlile, 2016

A Cataloguing-in-Publication entry is available from the catalogue of the National Library of Australia at www.nla.gov.au

ISBN-9781741175141

10 9 8 7 6 5 4 3 2 1

Printed and bound in China by 1010 Printing International Ltd

Publisher's note: Every effort has been made to ensure that the information in this book is accurate at the time of going to press. The publisher welcomes information and suggestions for correction or improvement.

Publisher's disclaimer: The publisher cannot accept responsibility for any errors or omissions. Please check regulations for projects in public spaces with your local authority. Always make sure items you find in nature are safe to use.